UNIVERSITY OF
WOLVERHAMPTON
KNOWLEDGE • INNOVATION • ENTERPRISE

Harrison Learning Centre
City Campus
University of Wolverhampton
St. Peter's Square
Wolverhampton
WV1 1RH
Telephone: 0845 408 1631
Online Renewals: www.wlv.ac.uk/lib/myaccount

Telephone Renewals: 01902 321333 or 0845 408 1631
Online Renewals: www.wlv.ac.uk/lib/myaccount
Please return this item on or before the last date shown above.
Fines will be charged if items are returned late.

D0182814

Historic Preservation

Collective Memory and Historical Identity

DIANE BARTHEL

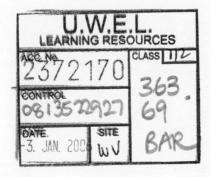
Rutgers University Press
New Brunswick, New Jersey

Publication of *Historic Preservation* was supported by a grant from the Graham Foundation for Advanced Studies in the Fine Arts.

All photographs courtesy of Diane Barthel.

Library of Congress Cataloging-in-Publication Data

Barthel, Diane L., 1949–
    Historic Preservation : collective memory and historical identity / Diane Barthel.
    p cm.
    Includes bibliographical references (p.) and index.
    ISBN 0-8135-2292-7 (cloth : alk. paper). — ISBN 0-8135-2293-5 (pbk. : alk. paper)
    1. Historic preservation—United States. 2. Historic preservation—Great Britain. 3. United States—Historiography. 4. Great Britain—Historiography. 5. Nationalism—United States. 6. Nationalism—Great Britain. 7. Group identity—United States. 8. Group identity—Great Britain. I. Title.
E159.B275   1996
363.6'9'0973—dc20
                                           95-53795
                                              CIP

British Cataloging-in-Publication information available

Manufactured in the United States of America

CONTENTS

Illustrations may be found between pages 100 and 101.

ACKNOWLEDGMENTS

I first became interested in historic preservation during my field research in the Amana Colonies, Iowa, and so my first debt is to the Amana people who expressed their perceptions and concerns about the need for and/or impact of preservation on their historic community. I am also indebted to the Martin Centre for Architecture and Urban Studies, Cambridge University, and the Department of Sociology, Essex University, where I was able to discuss the project with both British sociologists and British architects. This resulted in a better appreciation of cross-Atlantic differences in approaches to preservation. I would especially like to thank Professors Joseph Rykwert and Dalibor Vesely for allowing me to sit in on their year-long Master of Philosophy seminar in architectural theory, and my colleagues at Essex, including Leonore Davidoff, David Lee, Ken Plummer, David Rose, and Paul Thompson. I also had a very useful correspondence with David Lowenthal, who has written extensively and perceptively on preservation.

My colleagues at SUNY–Stony Brook were a wonderful resource: I especially thank the organizers and members of the Wednesday seminar for the chance to test out ideas. Students in my graduate Sociology of Culture classes were the source of many new ideas and useful exchanges. I very much enjoyed the opportunity of presenting a talk on industrial preservation to the Department of Sociology at the University of Connecticut, Storrs. Historian Ruth Schwartz Cowan was an expert guide to issues of interest to historians of science and technology.

Colleagues active in the Sociology of Culture section and the Community and Urban Sociology section of the American Sociological Association were very helpful, and I'd especially like to thank Barry Schwartz, Gaye Tuchman, Suzanne Vromen, Vera Zolberg, David Hammon, and John Logan. I also benefited from the opportunity of presenting my work at Conferences on Social Theory, Politics, and the Arts, and enjoyed discussing shared interests with Adolf Ehrentraut, who has done very interesting studies on preservation issues in Austria and Japan.

Curators, preservation professionals, and activists on both sides of the Atlantic gave generously of their time and expertise. The considerable expense of trans-Atlantic travel and research was lessened substantially by a travel grant awarded by the New York State Union of University Professors and a summer stipend from the National Endowment for the Humanities.

Marlie Wasserman expressed enthusiasm for this project from its inception, and Leslie Mitchner, her successor as Editor in Chief at Rutgers University Press, did a superb job of guiding it through the later stages of rewriting, editing, and production.

From start to finish, David Bouchier shared much of the research experience. With me, he visited enough agrarian villages and stately homes, industrial ruins and restored abbeys, war monuments and media reconstructions, to last several life times. Despite the occasional sense of "déjà vu all over again," he supported me fully in this endeavor. While I alone am responsible for whatever is lacking, the book itself could not exist without him, and so he bears the burden of another book dedication: to David, with thanks for being there, in so many ways.

An earlier version of chapter 2, Symbolic Bankers and Cultural Capital first appeared in the March 1989 issue of *Sociological Forum,* under the title "Historic Preservation: A Comparative Analysis."

An earlier version of chapter 3, Back to Utopia, first appeared in the fall 1990 issue of *Politics, Culture and Society* under the title "Nostalgia for America's Village Past: Staged Symbolic Communities," and was reprinted under the title "Back to Utopia: Staged Symbolic Communities" in *The Ethnic Quest for Community: Searching for Roots in the Lonely Crowd*, edited by Michael W. Hughey and Arthur J. Vidich (Greenwich, Conn.: JAI Press, 1993).

Historic Preservation

The Preservation ▨ CHAPTER 1
Project

'A Little Piece of Denmark,' 'a taste of Germany,' 'a touch of Holland,' . . . 'an antique city,' 'a quilt city,' 'a frontier village,' 'a journey into the past,' 'a county relics village.' Is this Disneyland? No, it's Iowa.
— Engler, "Drive-Thru History"

In Colorado there are several gold rush towns that compete to attract tourist visitors. Central City is one of these, with costumed characters strolling in front of Western-front structures and depicting the familiar frontier characters of cowboy, gambler, and whorehouse madam. One of the town's attractions is a perfectly preserved, late-Victorian house, left remarkably intact. It displays massive Victorian furniture, fussy faded wallpaper and floor coverings, and is absolutely crammed with knickknacks, gewgaws, and sentimental kitsch. It was not until I saw this representation of everyday Victoriana in what was then a cultural backwater that I understood in an immediate, visceral sense, why a whole generation of artists and architects reviled Victorian design. In its place they proposed modernism, which sought to banish kitsch and raise up humanity by clarifying and purifying design, by replacing accidental history and accumulated tradition with the rationalizing spirit of science and technology.

The irony is, of course, that it was only through an example of the Preservation Project that I could understand the modernist project. The Preservation Project is an attempt to revalue and re-present the past through saving, maintaining, and/or reconstructing historic structures and artifacts, and through heightening public awareness of their significance with local, regional, and/or national history.

Through preserving the past, the modernist desire to erase the past became clear; the passion behind the modernist creed appeared as more than opportunistic rhetoric or mere careerism. It appeared as a necessary and revolutionary force. The impression was reinforced by a visit to the Gropius House, in Lincoln, Massachusetts. There one could see an exemplar of the modernist project, before it became compromised and trivialized.

The Gropius House is one of the thirty-four structures owned by the Society for the Preservation of New England Antiquities. What would the early modernists, including Gropius, have said about their revolutionary achievements becoming part of the historical record? Their breakthrough exemplars are now museum pieces, revealing of their time, but no more or less guidelines for the future than Georgian townhouses.

Would they have an ironic appreciation for the fact that Colonial Williamsburg is being seriously proposed as a model for rebuilding and reforming American communities? Belgian architect Leon Krier was the first to propose this, but the idea has become part of an accepted vogue promoted by architects and planners across the States. On the other side of the Atlantic, modernists might be less surprised by Prince Charles's efforts to restore the architecture and visual integrity of the English countryside to his particular romanticized vision.

The point is that historic structures are a tangible form of evidence of the past and are thus a resource that should not be wasted or treated casually or negligently. Their very tangibility separates them from historic texts and media representations. People visit historic sites in large measure to "get in touch with history." Like research scientists who demand to see experimental results with their own eyes before they will believe them, visitors to historic sites want to see history with their own eyes.[1] They want to see Churchill's library and studio. They want to see where Lee's army was turned back at Gettysburg. They want to see historic Washington and London, Saugus and Ironbridge, rather than looking at someone else's slides or the pictures in a book.

Like any other project, the Preservation Project began with people who perceived a need for social change and who banded together to try to make it happen. They did this for their own reasons, whether self-serving or public-spirited.

At some point, however, preservation activists, like any activists, had to sell their idea to a broader public. They had to devise more explicit justifications for the proposed change. These explicit justifications are ideologies—complex arguments about the way the world should be. These ideologies are meant to extend beyond mere self or class interests, even if they always in some measure reflect their social class origins.

We can think of specific preservation projects or campaigns to save or restore this or that structure as forming part of a larger, ongoing Preservation Project. As a self-conscious cause, the Preservation Project dates back to the mid-nineteenth century. It was in large part a response to industrialization: its social dislocations and discontents. It assumed different forms in different contexts, as its justifying ideologies were tailored to respond to different cultural and social class patterns.

Great Britain and the United States provide for a particularly interesting and revealing comparison of how the one Preservation Project was adapted to suit these two different social contexts. Both nations share a common language and Anglo-centric culture. In Britain, however, social class is much more tightly structured and publicly acknowledged. It is an ever-present, institutionalized fact of life, down to which section of a pub you drink in and which train car you sit in. The British may rise or fall in social class position, but they find it harder to lose the more inbred signs of their social class origins, most notably accent, but extending across the whole range of habits, tastes, and demeanors.

In America, by contrast, social class is less tightly structured and less openly represented as a divisive force. Most Americans identify as middle class rather than upper or working class. The social leveling tendencies that Alexis de Tocqueville described following his visit to America in 1830 are alive today in the American ideology of equality, even as social status competition is an ever-present fact of life, and relative wealth and poverty visible on every streetscape. In America, one is not meant to put on accents or airs, or even "to have an attitude." Equality of opportunity suggests that no difference is or should be so fundamental that it cannot be overcome, and success stories abound in popular literature and media to drive the point home.

Partly because of the social class structure and partly because of cultural differences, the Preservation Project has assumed a different organizational structure in Great Britain than in the United States. While Britain has many local groups and history enthusiasts, much preservation work is accomplished through two powerful national organizations. The National Trust for Places of Historic Interest or Natural Beauty, founded in 1895, currently has partial or complete ownership of over two hundred houses and parks and protects more than six hundred thousand acres of countryside. Its sister organization, the National Trust for Scotland, similarly dominates the Preservation Project in Scotland, with over one hundred structures and one hundred thousand acres of countryside in its care. English Heritage's properties span some four thousand years, and include such nationally significant properties as Stonehenge and Lindisfarne. In Britain there is also a national system for the ranking of properties of historic significance, which ranking has powers of enforcement attached to it.

In the United States, no such top-down system exists; properties must be proposed for landmarking or to be part of historic districts by localities and states, and owners retain significant rights to prevent the process. While there were local and regional organizations from the mid-nineteenth century, no national organization was founded until the creation of the National Trust for Historic Preservation in 1951. Its holdings are much more restricted than its British counterpart: in 1994 the Trust had partial or complete control over eighteen historic sites. It functions more as an informational clearing house, sponsor of programs, participant in legal debates and controversies, and champion of local, state, and regional activism.

These differences will be more fully developed in chapter two. What is worth noting here is that the above differences in social class patterns and organizational structures have led to a third difference—one that is ideological. This pertains to what preservationists see as their purpose and elaborate as such to the broader public, upon whose support they rely.

In Britain, the upper classes have historically dominated the Preservation Project and continue to do so. In fact, much of what Americans term preservation is considered "conservation" in Britain. Conservation of structures is the highest responsibility; public access and education follow after it. Because of both the people involved and the explicit goals, the Preservation Project in Britain is associated with conservative political forces.

To its critics, British preservation appears to be the ideological activity of the ruling class, intent on promulgating an image of the past that never was and further abetting the process of national economic decline by refusing to make way for change. Sometimes the accusation is that the past is exploited for personal and class profit, rather than used to educate the public in its history. According to Robert Hewison, the "heritage industry" dishes out "bogus history" with little regard for authenticity, let alone conflicting class interpretations.[2] His compatriot Patrick Wright condemns what he calls "trafficking in history," with all immoral connotations left intact.[3]

To such charges, British preservationists have historically responded and continue to respond that their efforts are for neither individual gain nor class dominance, but rather for the benefit of the nation. Robin Fedden quotes British historian G. M. Trevalyan, "Without vision the people perish, and without national beauty the English people will perish in the spiritual sense." Fedden then goes on to state, "It is the Trust's first duty jealously to guard the spiritual resources of its lands, their quiet remoteness, and all that contributes to their beauty."[4] Thus the Trust exists to keep the British people and the British spirit alive.

As suggested above, the Preservation Project in the States has been less centralized. However, it still has historically had a White Anglo-Saxon Protestant cast to it, with the majority of its members and leaders drawn from the upper middle and upper classes. It has thus been open to charges of, if not "ruling class domination," as in Britain, then certainly social elitism. Responding to such charges in 1976, James Biddle, president of the National Trust, wrote in his introduction to *America's Forgotten Architecture* that the book "should put to rest forever that arbitrary habit of singling out environmentalists and preservationists as 'them'—the other side. There is only one environment out there, and what happens to it is not up to any vague or far-removed 'them,' but to *us*."[5]

Needless to say, neither the book nor Biddle's defense put the charges to rest, for they were far from arbitrary. In the 1980s and 1990s, the National Trust became much more proactive. It increasingly supported projects in ethnic and low-income neighborhoods, and promoted persons of color active in preservation. It made cultural pluralism a rallying cry. By contrast, British preservationists, when confronted by the issue of pluralism so strongly promoted in the United States, said they felt no need to preserve structures that were representative of the working class, or because they were significant within the Indian or West Indian communities, or on any grounds other than historical and/or architectural significance. Nor did they feel any need to recruit from a diversity of regional, ethnic, or class backgrounds, although the British Trust does maintain regional offices. The label of conservative seemed more descriptive of their goals than damning of their enterprise, which they emphasized meant preserving the very best, rather than the merely representative. Only recently have they begun to broaden their acquisitions to include, for example, Sutton House, a small country house in Hackney, East London; and Orford ness, five miles of Suffolk coast containing concrete pagodas where nuclear weapons were tested in the 1950s.

These differences in social class, organizational structure, and ideology shape the Preservation Projects in Great Britain and the United States. Rather than trying to cover all of preservation, I have focused on areas involving particular social issues and controversies of wide interest. Thus areas such as conservation techniques or the intricacies of preservation law, of interest largely to specialists, will be relatively ignored. Instead, I will focus on such issues as agrarian nostalgia, industrial representations, religious preservation, the politics of war commemoration, globalization of preservation, and the commercialization of historic structures and artifacts.

One common concern running throughout these different topics is authenticity. For preservationists, the historic structure must be interpreted accurately and in a context free of contaminating purposes or self-serving interpretations. Further, all decisions regarding the structure must be documented and must be reversible. Additions to structures must be distinguished from and not fundamentally change the original physical structure. Future generations of experts must be able to "read" what this generation has done and to undo it if necessary—all in the service of authenticity.

The public visits historic sites to see the evidence, to get in touch with history. Their encounter with history is not, however, an unproblematic one. The public implicitly accepts that what it sees is the real thing. But authenticity, as preservationists recognize, is an elusive goal. For example, the historic Huntington Hotel in Pasadena, California, was razed to the ground despite a concerted campaign waged by dedicated preservationists. In its stead, a brand new hotel was erected, nostalgically incorporating the earlier hotel's name, exterior appearance, and even specific architectural and interior features.

The public appeared delighted with this phoenix, much to the chagrin of editor Arnold Berke of *Historic Preservation News*, the newsletter of the National Trust for Historic Preservation. As he cautioned his colleagues, "The general public does not think of preservation as preservationists do—as the comprehensive practice of saving, preserving or restoring, reusing and interpreting a large and varied number of old buildings, structures, vessels, and sites. The public pictures preservation far more generally as a movement that tries to save landmarks." Coming to the point, he concluded, "The nature of those landmarks and of the preservation process is not something people dwell on."[6] It's the end result they care about, and whether what they see seems to do the job as a social marker as well as or better than what was there before.

A historic representation can be judged authentic or inauthentic on the basis of its site, structures, and content. Authenticity in the case of site can be defined as the original site; in the case of structure, as the original building (recognizing how authenticity is manipulated and redefined through processes of maintenance and restoration). In the case of content, authenticity is even more difficult to judge. Given the complexity of the issue, one tack is to emphasize motive, with authenticity defined as a concerted effort to achieve historically accurate representations. The ultimate historic "truth" of the representation may remain unknown, or may be revealed at a later time to be something quite different than imagined.

By these criteria, Disneyland is typical of one extreme of historic representations, insofar as it is constructed on an arbitrary site with new structures that make little pretense to historical accuracy, even as they call up historic images. By contrast, most of the historic houses administered by the National Trusts on both sides of the Atlantic are original structures on their original sites, into which great effort goes toward maximizing the authenticity of the representation's content.

In between these two extremes, there are many interesting permutations and combinations. Plimouth Plantation has nonoriginal structures on a nonauthentic site, but attempts nonetheless to achieve authenticity of content. Boscobel, in New York's Hudson Valley, is an authentic Federal-style house with authentic content, but was moved to a new site in order to be rescued and restored. Old Sturbridge Village, in Massachusetts, has culled authentic structures from all over New England and gathered them together on a site where no village existed previously. Colonial Williamsburg, by contrast, has both original structures and reconstructions on the original site.

Even where authenticity is an explicit goal, tourist facilities must be fitted into the historic frame. Room must be allotted for lavatories, parking lots, snack bars, and gift shops, whose stylistic integration is a standard problem for design professionals.

Authenticity can also be multilayered. Curators may continue to present representations they recognize as inauthentic, but which reveal an earlier period of curatorial connoisseurship. These representations are authentic to the understanding of a period, if not to the actual historic period represented. Such is the case with the Powel Room, a Philadelphia Colonial parlor on display at New York's Metropolitan Museum of Art. Specifically, both the hand-painted Chinese wallpaper and elaborately ornamented plaster ceiling are known to be inauthentic to the room, yet allowed to remain as "testimony to the taste of the 'colonial revival' of the 1920s, when it was installed at the Museum."

Secondly, curators may choose one authentic moment in a structure's history over other possible moments. The moment chosen may not necessarily be the most historically significant. It may instead be the moment for which the most extensive and attractive furnishings are available, or the moment which provides the most appealing tourist narrative. One restored Southern mansion has a family wedding as the moment around which interpretation will take place. A curious combination of historic moments is found in an eighteenth-century Colonial mansion that features a Colonial Revival dining room from the 1930s. The logic for preserving this room was that it was famous in its own right insofar as it has featured as an exemplar of that style in design magazines and textbooks.

As the latter example suggests, many historic buildings evolve over time. In *The Preservationist's Progress,* Hugh Howard chronicles the debate in one New York State town over whether a historic house should be restored to its pristine, early nineteenth-century condition, or left with later additions. These additions included a wide Victorian porch and, centered over it, a second-floor enclosed porch described as Adirondack vernacular.

When the town voted for the first option of complete restoration to the earliest incarnation, critics regretted what they perceived as the loss of the layering of time on the structure. "I think that there's a constant urge to make the old new . . . and restoration is often the easiest route," commented Chester Liebs. "It's sort of like surgery: it's easy to go in and cut."[7] Contemporary preservation philosophy is less enthusiastic about arbitrarily fixing one date or period to which a building or site's appearance is restored, and more prone toward accepting the complexity of time's traces.

Problems relating to authenticity arise even when structures do not evolve over time. In 1992, Long Island's futuristic Aluminaire House still had its original 1932 aluminum—now tarnished, dented, and pockmarked. As the preservationist coordinating the restoration argued, "There's a tension between wanting to save the historic materials and recreating the architects' original idea of a bright, shiny 'machine for living.' . . . If we don't use new aluminum, we don't provide the idea."[8] When given this example, a British conservationist commented that clearly the thing to do was to preserve the tarnished Aluminaire House, to show the way it actually looked, and build a new Aluminaire House alongside it, to show the way it *should* look.

Given these considerations, determining absolute authenticity becomes a more metaphysical than practical exercise. What is more productive is to understand what the different social actors—preservationists, politicians, developers, publics—think is authentic and why authenticity matters to them, if, indeed, it does matter. Historic structures may be resources for shaping collective memories, but what we make of them is up to us. The Preservation Project serves to remind us, after all, that Vico was right: History is not God-given, it is humanly made. And what was once socially constructed can be socially reconstructed, through interpretation.

Symbolic ▨ CHAPTER 2
Bankers and
Cultural Capital

January 27–29: Annapolis Heritage Antiques
Show, to benefit London Town Founda-
tion, Maryland.
January 1-April 30: "Castles in the Sand":
The Design of Long Island's State Parks . .
. . presented by the Society for the Preser-
vation of Long Island Antiquities. The
Gallery, Cold Spring Harbor, New York.
February 19: Masked Victorian Ball aboard
the Queen Mary, sponsored by Victorian
Society of Heritage House, Fullerton, Cal-
ifornia.   —Calendar items from
                    Historic Preservation,
                    January/February 1995

Chances are that the people who attended the above antiques
show, gallery exhibit, or Victorian ball did not represent a
random sample of the local population. Much research suggests that
people attracted to such cultural events are drawn disproportion-
ately from middle- and upper-class backgrounds.[1] They may have
cultivated long-term interests in antiques or local history. Or they
may have wished to add new areas of expertise while enjoying a
pleasant social activity surrounded by like-minded people.

Culture has been seen as a kind of capital that individuals can build up and trade on. Engaging in cultural activities such as visiting art museums or attending operas and demonstrating cultural knowledge, for example, knowing the difference between Manet and Monet, are all forms of cultural capital.[2] Because of one's class position and family background, one develops a set of tastes, outlooks, attitudes, and habits which, as French sociologist Pierre Bourdieu argues, must be invested in the right cultural activities. These, in turn, provide the right sort of status indicators, which reflect back upon the person.

But the issue is more complex. If culture is capital, it can be invested in many things, not just individual class and status position. There are also ongoing processes of legitimation and delegitimation of meanings and values. How much capital attaches to attending a play or buying a painting depends on what is in vogue among a certain group. There is a changing market for culture in which the value of an object or experience is constantly being adjusted by changes in supply and demand. The process of legitimation attached to these changes must be viewed as problematic in its own right. People in other social classes also trade cultural capital in other forms, such as rock music and sports knowledge, to gain status within their social groups.

Kenneth Burke provides a somewhat broader perspective than that of Bourdieu. He begins with the recognition that symbol creating is an essential human characteristic. From this process, he argues, there may emerge specific "symbolic bankers." As Burke writes, "A complex symbolism is a kind of 'spiritual currency'—and a group of 'bankers' may arise who manipulate this medium of exchange to their special benefits."[3]

Historic preservation has emerged as an appropriate activity for the investing of cultural capital, with the expectation of personal gain in status and financial terms. Beyond such direct benefits to the individuals involved, the preservation movement had to claim more widespread benefits in order to gain social acceptance as a worthy cause. This claiming is similar to the social legitimation attached to other activities supported in large measure by the upper classes, such as arts support and other forms of philanthropy. The people involved in these activities like to see themselves as performing a public good, whether the public appreciates it or not.

Thus cultural activities can benefit both the individuals directly involved and society at large, although such is not by any means assured. The relationship between personal interest and social interest is, in fact, a highly charged one. In reviewing the development of historic preservation in the United States and Great Britain, we see how different attitudes and motives have figured in preservation campaigns, and how preservation was legitimated through appeal to several distinct societal values.

▨ *Preservation in Britain*

The origins of preservation in Great Britain were primarily intellectual and artistic. Thinkers as different as Edmund Burke and William Cobbett shared a common revulsion at many of the physical and social changes industrialization was producing across Britain.[4] In his *Rural Rides,* published in 1830, Cobbett described the beauty of the English countryside, a beauty formed not just of physical landscape but of the traditional way of life attached to it: the customs and social understandings that were as much responsible for its shape and aspect as any natural feature, any stand of trees or rocky promontory.

Writers and artists, particularly those associated with the Romantic Movement, not only found beauty in nature, they also perceived truth and nobility in an earlier social age—the Medieval period—that they then contrasted to the social disorder of their own times. According to historian Charles Dellheim, "They saw in the Middle Ages a source of values that represented alternatives to the emergent industrial capitalist social order. In Gothic architecture they saw the highest expression of the human quest for the infinite and delight in the finite. The Middle Ages provided them with an exemplar of spiritual devotion and religious piety that was profoundly appealing to those who craved both but often possessed neither."[5]

One major result of their writings and expressed concern was the founding, by John Ruskin, John Stuart Mill, William Morris, and others, of the Commons Preservation Society in 1865. The purpose of this society was to help protect the remaining communally held lands against enclosure, with campaigns launched to defend such notable lands as Hampstead Heath and Wimbledon Common.[6] A second major effort resulted in the founding of the Society for the Protection of Ancient Buildings in 1877. This group protested the careless restoration and alteration of historic buildings and monuments.

For Ruskin, the chief justification for conservation was contained within the idea of age itself: the quasi-sacred character of that which has endured through generations of inhabitants and successions of historical events.[7] Other members of this artistic intellectual coterie went further than Ruskin. Morris in particular saw preservation as part of a battle against an increasingly commercialized and secular world. "Is it absolutely necessary," he asked in *Commonweal* on 6 August 1887, "that every scrap of space in the City should be devoted to money-making, and are religion, sacred memories, recollections of the great dead, memorials of the past, works of England's greatest architects to be banished from this wealthy city?"[8]

The widening of interest from the Medieval period to the "ancient" per se was accompanied by a widening of support from artists and intellectuals to a broader base in local communities. During the Victorian period, local organizations sprang up throughout England, many of them combining an interest in historic monuments with interests in natural history, antiques, or archaeology: for example, the Dorset Natural History and Antiquarian Field Club (1875), the Derbyshire Archaeological and Natural History Society (1878), and the Hampstead Antiquarian and Historical Society (1897).[9]

This spreading interest in the past laid the groundwork for the foundation of the National Trust in 1895. Three individuals provided the specific catalyst. Robert Hunter, a solicitor active in the Commons Preservation Society, suggested in a speech in Birmingham made to the National Association for the Promotion of Social Science that a "land company" might be formed "with a view to the protection of public interests in the open spaces of the country."[10] This suggestion was quickly seconded by Octavia Hill, a philanthropist active in improving housing for the urban poor. She suggested to Hunter that the term "company" might be changed to "trust," commenting, "You will do better . . . to bring forward its benevolent than its commercial character. People don't like unsuccessful business, but do like Charity where a little money goes a long way because of good management."[11] The third main actor, Canon Hardwicke Rawnsley, had helped defend the scenic Lake District against a railway bill, but had initially appeared uninterested in the trust. In 1893, however, when certain Lake District properties of scenic value came on the market, he recognized that a need existed for an agency that could buy, manage, and protect such scenic and historic sites. He then joined with Hill and Hunter to protect the Lake District. This, then, became the first important symbol of British preservation, as the call to "Save the Lake District" drew support from the many who had vacationed there and who saw this mountainous area as a land of exceptional natural beauty with an almost spiritual dimension.

The fight was to preserve this preindustrial landscape from the forces of industrialization, a challenge the leadership had already faced in the effort to preserve common land. To be effective in this battle, however, they realized they must adopt a new form of social organization. In industrial society, the sporadic resistance of concerned individuals would not suffice. Thus in January 1895, the National Trust for Places of Historic Interest or Natural Beauty was incorporated as a public, nonprofit company.[12]

In the early decades there was a real sense of adventure to this new cause, and a spirit of camaraderie among those involved. As one example, former Trust official Robin Fedden recounts the exploits of "Ferguson's Gang" which, beginning in the 1930s, revolved around raising funds and rescuing buildings. "Elected by secret ballot, the members of this saintly mafia were anonymous to the world, and assumed such colorful pseudonyms as Sister Agatha, Kate O'Brien, the Nark, Bill Stickers, the Bloody Bishop, and Red Biddy." Their cash contributions to the Trust were all delivered in notes and coins (usually Victorian) by a masked member of the gang. "No questions were asked, much less answered."[13]

In 1900, Trust membership stood at approximately 250 members. By 1928 it had grown to over 1,000, and by 1935 the figure was over 8,000. The biggest growth occurred after World War II. In 1950 membership was 23,000; in 1960, 97,000; and by 1965, 158,000.[14] In 1992, almost a century after its founding, the National Trust counted over 2 million members.[15] As typically happens in the history of organizations and associations, some old-timers regret the very success of their movement in terms of numbers attracted. Recalling the period of growth in the Trust's postwar years, Robin Fedden wrote, "It was to be a period of gain, but also, in one sense, of loss":

> Size and a more formal administration meant that the Trust became less personal and contacts with donors and tenants less intimate. . . . A dedicated and amateur group, quixotic and sometimes haphazard, was replaced by an organization. This change to meet changed circumstances was necessary, but all who served the Trust before the war recognize that something was lost. They would echo the sentiments of someone who worked for the Trust with little consideration of personal reward for over twenty years: "The times when things were smaller, more amateur, more voluntary, produced a wonderful feeling . . . there was a bond between everyone concerned."[16]

In the early years, the small but dedicated membership was very successful in acquiring scenic lands and grand historic buildings. By 1900 they had acquired 180 properties, including the Farne Islands, large stretches of the Lake District, Bodiam and Tatteshall Castles, Chedworth Roman villa, and Barrington Court, among others. Along with such successes, preservationists faced continued challenges from industrialization, commercialization, and new leisure activities. Trust committee minutes record threats to the landscape due to motor rallies on the South Downs, hydroplanes on Lake Windermere, pylons, advertising, new highways, and pollution attacking many sites of natural beauty and historic significance.[17]

Initially the Trust appeared eager to accept any property of historic merit or scenic beauty, but eventually it was forced to become more selective, emphasizing that properties would have to be of national significance. Most notably, in the years surrounding World War II they undertook what is known as the "Country House Scheme." The large country estates, which had symbolized the leisured good life for the upper classes, had become increasingly difficult to maintain in the post–World War I years, as the number of servants declined and as death duties were imposed on the estates. For many owners threatened with having to give up family estates, the Trust came to the rescue. Through this procedure, descendants maintained ownership of their impressive properties, receiving Trust financial support in exchange for opening parts of their homes to tourists during limited seasonal hours. These country homes have become symbolic of the Trust among whose holdings they figure prominently.

Post World War II, the National Trust continued to expand the number and scope of its activities. As many as thirty properties a year became Trust holdings in this period of rapid growth and development. This was an era of planning, both in response to a new emphasis on social planning in government and as a result of the expansion in Trust properties. As the Trust developed in size, a more formal administration was set in place. New government legislation regarding death duties encouraged the flow of country house properties into Trust care, including such notable properties as Petworth (1947), Ickworth (1956), and Saltram (1957). In 1945, the Trust's Country Houses Committee was replaced by the Historic Buildings Committee, which worked in close contact with government departments. By the same year, a system of regional offices staffed with regional agents had begun taking shape.[18]

The changing scope of Trust concerns in the postwar years was reflected in the creation of a Gardens Scheme in 1948. Comparable to the Country House Scheme, this program led to the preservation of such major gardens as Hidcote, Nymans, Bodnant, and Sheffield Park. Interest also expanded in the relatively neglected field of industrial preservation. While the National Trust had some industrial holdings prior to this period, they were chosen in part for their picturesque appeal, as in the preservation of the cotton mill and village at Styal, Cheshire. In the late 1950s and 60s, a wider range of factories, bridges, mills, and canals were preserved.[19]

Today, the National Trust owns more than 570,000 acres, making it Britain's largest private landowner. It also holds protective covenants on another 78,000 acres. Its properties include over 200 houses, including 88 country houses and 43 houses associated with famous people. In addition, there are 50 villages and hamlets under Trust management, 114 gardens, as well as preindustrial and Roman antiquities, wind and water mills, industrial sites, nature reserves, parks, and vast stretches of countryside. The Trust's annual budget exceeds 80 million pounds (approximately 130–150 million dollars), with income received from an array of investments, government grants, memberships and fees, sales, bequests and legacies.

With its headquarters in Edinburgh, the National Trust for Scotland exists as a separate entity. Founded in 1931, its membership now stands at over 250,000. Like the National Trust, this organization is dedicated to the preservation of "lands and buildings of historic interest or natural beauty for the benefit of the nation." It owns 100,000 acres of countryside and more than 100 properties. These properties include a weaver's cottage near Glasgow; a tenement house, also in Glasgow; most of the sacred island of Iona, Kellie Castle and garden in Fife; Charles Rennie Mackintosh's "The Hill House," in Helensburgh, Strathclyde; and Carlyle's birthplace, in Ecclefechan, in Dumfries and Galloway. This short list only hints at the variety of properties owned.

Another major force in British preservation, English Heritage is a quasi-autonomous, nonincorporated government organization, or "quango." Founded in 1984, English Heritage is held "responsible for securing the preservation of England's architectural and archaeological heritage" and for protecting "the public's enjoyment and knowledge of the heritage through its management of approximately four hundred monuments and buildings." Many of these structures were formally under the care of the Secretary of State for the Environment. They range from major monuments such as Bodiam Castle and Battle Abbey to small churches and archaeological sites.

A third organization with a more activist mandate is SAVE Britain's Heritage. Founded in 1975, SAVE is a pressure group with about two hundred members who campaign for the "preservation and re-use of historic buildings, gardens and landscapes." Besides getting involved in specific issues, it publishes a wide range of reports on specific types of threatened buildings. In the past, it opposed a plan by the Church of England to rid itself of redundant churches, and, more recently, spoke out against a controversial proposal by English Heritage to perform a triage among its properties, cutting out those that were neither popular nor profitable by turning their care over to other, usually local, authorities.

Other organizations, such as the Twentieth Century Society (formerly the Thirties Society, founded in 1979), the Victorian Society (founded 1958), and the Georgian Group (founded 1937), focus on structures of specific periods. There are also societies for industrial preservation, including among them the Brewery History Society, the Industrial Locomotive Society, and the Peak District Mines Historical Society. Since the nineteenth century local societies have been popular. At present, there are at least eighty-eight County Archaeological Societies, seventeen County Historical Records Societies, and twenty-four general Archaeological Societies, including antiquarian associations. Many of these local societies take an interest in the preservation and/or maintenance of historic sites.

Thus there is continuing strong support for preservation in Britain, represented both by powerful governmental and non-governmental organizations and by a wealth of local societies and interest groups. At the same time, there is mounting opposition to preservationists spreading their net of control over a growing number and range of structures. As structures from the more recent past, including modernist houses and office blocks come under consideration, critics wonder whether the nation will become over-preserved, and whether the potential for private initiative and innovation will be stifled.

Preservation in the United States

In America, the motive behind the earliest preservation effort was neither artistic nor intellectual: it was patriotic. The first major effort was the successful crusade, launched by South Carolinian Ann Pamela Cunningham in 1853, to save Mount Vernon. Her purpose was to inspire in future generations the patriotism and notable characters of the Founding Fathers. To some extent, her Mount Vernon Ladies Association formed the prototype for other early organizations, such as the Daughters of the American Revolution and the Colonial Dames. Such organizations usually limited their preservation efforts to one building for each chapter, often used as the local headquarters.

Other sites with a clearly patriotic symbolism for early preservationists included Andrew Jackson's home, The Hermitage (saved in 1856); Carpenter's Hall, site of the First Continental Congress (also 1856); Washington's headquarters in Morristown, New Jersey (1873); and Valley Forge (1878).[20] Local historical societies were formed throughout the later nineteenth and early twentieth centuries, many of them specifically to honor the place where Washington rested his head, or where some native son of later prominence had passed his early years.

While patriotism was the major motive behind many nineteenth-century preservationist efforts, it was soon joined by an economic motive. This second motive also reveals the extent to which preservation must be seen as a culturally specific response to industrialization. The most forceful proponents of this second, twentieth-century message were the major industrialists. Chief among them were John D. Rockefeller, who provided funding for the restoration of Colonial Williamsburg, and Henry Ford who created Greenfield Village in 1929 to present his own version of history to the American public.

Up through 1930, there was little thought of a national organization. The six states of New England were already joined together in the Society for the Preservation of New England Antiquities (SPNEA), founded in 1910. Under the direction of William Sumner Appleton, an architectural historian and full-time preservationist, the SPNEA shifted the focus from patriotism to architecture in its campaigns.[21] Elsewhere, specific cities and towns became centers of preservation. Not surprisingly, these were most often places with a definite sense of identity shared either by a local upper class or by a new status group of recent arrivals.

One example is Charleston, South Carolina, where the decline following the Civil War had left fine old ante-bellum buildings threatened with demolition by the early twentieth century. Following the example set by Ann Cunningham, Susan Pringle Frost, a real estate broker, began a crusade to save these buildings. Unlike Cunningham, she began by restoring them and selling them, often at a loss. Her interest in preserving homes with the "stability and nobility of character and taste, which a modern commercial age can ill afford to dispense with," soon spread to other influential Charlestonians, as Hosmer is at pains to point out—"evenly divided between men and women, with professionals from many important fields"—who shared a belief "that something was sacred about the city"[22]

While each local crusade had its specific symbols and goals based in large measure on its historic legacy, the crusaders did seem drawn from the same pool. Ministers were notable among preservation's leadership on both sides of the Atlantic, and women were also well represented. Once the professionals—in those decades almost by definition men—became involved, the proportion of women declined. In both settings, teachers and artists were also among the first to recognize the potential in neglected byways of history. In San Antonio, a small group of women artists founded the San Antonio Conservation Society. Other notable centers of early preservationist activism included Natchez, where women's garden clubs organized annual pilgrimages to historic homes "Where the Old South Still Lives": St. Augustine, New Orleans, Monterey, Annapolis, Newport, and old Western mining towns such as Tombstone, Arizona.[23]

Up until 1930, Federal involvement in preservation was minimal, about evenly split between the War Department, responsible for monuments and battlefields, and the National Park Service (NPS). In the 1930s, however, the NPS began to assert a greater authority, demonstrated in particular by winning support for the Historic American Buildings Survey. While providing government work for unemployed architects, this survey documented the architectural structure and detail of historic buildings, many of which were at risk. The survey itself provided a pathway for communication among experts, while it alerted the public to preservation possibilities within their own communities. The second major achievement of the NPS was the passage of the Historic Sites Act in 1935. This act set the terms for the acquisition of properties, called for a survey of properties to be repeated at least every ten years, and recommended a National Board on Historic Sites to advise the Secretary of the Interior.

Still, the NPS was not an independent agency. When President Roosevelt turned against preservation at America's entry into World War II, preservationists realized that the full responsibility for existing and future properties might be better handled by an organization separate from government that could make preservation its one goal and raison d'être. Further, the localism that had characterized American preservation from the beginning made coordination very difficult. It was for these reasons that professionals and activists in government and in the private sector founded the National Trust for Historic Preservation in 1949. Modeled on the British Trust, it was to be a private, nonprofit organization dedicated to preserving America's historic legacy and to furthering the preservationist cause.

Fifty-five years behind the British Trust, the American Trust has far fewer properties and assets. The American National Trust operates only eighteen historic homes open to the public, ranging from southern plantations to the homes of Woodrow Wilson and Frank Lloyd Wright. This compares to over one hundred historic homes operated by the British Trust. Much of the American organization's emphasis is on encouraging local groups, offering technical advice, and lobbying for preservationist causes in state and national governments.

While both the British National Trust and English Heritage deny having a political agenda, seeing instead their mission as focused on conserving and interpreting, the American Trust has embraced a political agenda extending beyond these two functions. This is evident in their "mission statement," which reads: "The mission of the National Trust for Historic Preservation is to foster an appreciation of the diverse character and meaning of our American cultural heritage and to preserve and revitalize the livability of our communities by leading the nation in saving America's historic environments."[24] The key phrases in this statement are "diverse character" and "livability of our communities." The issue of cultural diversity is of great importance to American preservation in the 1990s and is worth special consideration.

▨ Cultural Diversity

Whereas preservation in the United States once had a definite "Daughters of the American Revolution" cast, today it is not hard to find counter examples, all designed to promote and to celebrate America's diverse cultural and ethnic heritage. Boston, where millions of tourists have followed the Freedom Trail to sites of revolutionary significance, now also has a Black Heritage Trail.[25] Among the fourteen sites featured are the early-nineteenth-century Abiel Smith School and the African Meeting House, the oldest existing African-American church in the nation.

Chicago has eight structures of significance to the African-American community listed in the National Register under the thematic title of the Black Metropolis. Included among these are the Eighth Regiment Armory and the Wabash Avenue YMCA. Many historic structures of New York's Harlem have been designated landmarks, and a slaves' burial ground was recently discovered in lower Manhattan. Its preservation and interpretation quickly became a top priority of the New York Landmarks Preservation Commission.

Across the river in Brooklyn, the Weeksville African-American Museum interprets the history of the African-American community for schoolchildren and other visitors. In Washington, D.C. and elsewhere, former segregated schoolhouses have been preserved. Perhaps the most notable among these is the Topeka, Kansas, schoolhouse from which came the challenge to the "separate but equal" basis for school segregation, struck down by the Supreme Court in *Brown v. the Board of Education.*

Where once only grand, ante-bellum mansions were thought worthy of preservation, now great interest is exhibited toward the preservation of slave quarters, as at sites in the Carolinas and at Carter's Grove, outside of Williamsburg, Virginia.

Mexico and the United States are joining together to promote a "Heritage Corridor" along the lower Rio Grande/Rio Bravo. California has a wealth of historic sites of significance to minority populations, including the Watts Towers and Chinatown, and Georgia publishes a guide to African-American sites within the state called *Historic Black Resources*. Across the nation, cultural diversity is generating a new sense of excitement shared by many people active in preservation.

Minority sites are creating a preservation boomlet in part because they solve two of the fundamental problems facing preservation: namely, the perpetual search for new sites and new types of sites to save, and the need to counter charges of elitism and to demonstrate public service to all segments of the population.

Preservationists are motivated by the fact that by the year 2000 minorities will represent one third of the American population.[26] This predicted and sizable population can either support or reject preservationist proposals. Longtime preservation activist Antoinette Lee is well aware of the changing population profile and encourages fellow preservationists to dance to the new tune in a new rhythm. "There is little that traditional architectural and historical analysis can bring to a purely functional building, such as the Eden Center in Falls Church, Virginia, where a significant Vietnamese community has concentrated its businesses and social and cultural activities." She suggests instead that such structures would be better served if more social historians, anthropologists, and ethnographers became active in the preservation process.

Others question the open embrace of all ethnic structures, whatever their intrinsic and/or architectural merit. David Lowenthal, for one, argues that preservation is neither the only nor necessarily the best means of celebrating ethnic heritage and diversity: "Polish American, Greek American, African American physical realms are not ethnically distinctive in recognizably Old World ways; many Chinatowns are little more than Hollywood variants; most native American villages forget or forgo ancestral forms." He continues, "It is vital to celebrate local diversity. But for minority impress, we must look to other realms of culture—worship, foods, social traits, the arts. There, more than in building or landscape, ethnic America displays a dynamic living heritage."[27]

Clearly, it depends in part on how you justify preservation. Some stress the internal merit of the structure, others emphasize external criteria, including significance to the collective memory of a given ethnic group, and still others argue for a combination of both sets of criteria. A mundane building may be highly significant to collective memory and deemed worthy of preservation or reconstruction.

American preservation organizations have also become concerned not just with preserving structures representing cultural diversity, but with integrating a culturally diverse group of people within their ranks. Beginning in 1991, cultural diversity was explicitly part of the American National Trust's agenda.

The Trust holds an annual convention which gathers its own members, representatives from the Washington preservation establishment and from State Historical Preservation Offices, among many other interested parties. Running about five days, the whole affair has the feeling of a revival camp meeting, with leaders trying to reinspire followers with a sense of high purpose and allegiance to the cause.

In 1992, the national meetings were held in Miami with the unifying theme of "Fostering Appreciation for Cultural Diversity." By selecting this focus, Trust officials hoped "to lay to rest the ill-informed criticisms that paint preservation as an elitist's avocation."[28] Featured speakers included Harvey B. Gantt, the first African-American mayor of Charlotte, N.C.; Linda Chavez, the Hispanic former head of the U.S. Commission on Civil Rights; Dr. Scott Momaday, a Native-American Pulitzer-prize–winning author; and Representative John Lewis of Georgia, an African-American and early Civil Rights activist.

The approximately two thousand conference participants could also attend smaller sessions including "Preservation Strategies for the African-American Church," "Identifying and Documenting Cultural Diversity for the National Register," and "Preserving American Indian Cultures." At the closing plenary session a trustee presented a list of goals for achieving cultural diversity, including such well-intentioned ideals as "appreciate the fact that preservation of our culturally diverse heritage creates self-esteem and a sense of pride in people and place," and "appreciate the tradition of cultural diversity in American society and the unifying force of this continuing tradition in our nation's future."[29]

With the 1992 Rodney King trial and the Los Angeles riots still fresh in everyone's mind, these goals reflected the triumph of hope over recent experience. For the time being, the idea of preservation overcoming racial prejudice and economic inequality and thereby becoming a unifying force in more than words remains a highly dubious proposition.

Whether or not cultural diversity in preservation can solve major problems of prejudice and inequality, it is likely to create new problems and conundrums. For example, professional preservationists accept the principle of rewarding amateur participation, and try to be open to local ideas. This long-held principle was made explicit in the 1992 annual meeting goals, which included "Acknowledge that cultural groups have a right to define their own cultural values and the means by which these values will be preserved and interpreted."[30] But preservationists also owe allegiance to their professional knowledge and standards. This expert knowledge and these standards are the source of their status and livelihood. Somehow, they must either sell the community on their ideas, and/or subtly incorporate local ideas without losing professional control.

Professionals working in the field acknowledge their frustration when local planning boards and other review committees reject their suggestions. For example, preservationists tend to favor techniques that clearly show what part of a structure is original, and what parts are reconstructed or imaginatively recreated. The authentic must be clearly distinguishable from the inauthentic. In a variety of contexts, locals have preferred to create a harmonious and pleasing whole, strict authenticity be damned. Museum contributions may also be more valued locally for who gave them than for their strict historic or thematic value.

Where true cultural diversity exists, it is likely to create a conflict of interpretive means and standards between local residents and more cosmopolitan professionals. The other possibility is that the preservation profession may come to enjoy cultural diversity among its ranks at the same time that it achieves cultural hegemony over the process of interpretation. This could very well lead to a "bureaucratization of the spirit," as all involved come to share the same, highly professionalized approach to what is to be preserved and how it is to be presented to the public.[31]

Indeed, some would say we are there already. Our encounters with the past are becoming increasingly managed for us. We are less likely to get the actual history *wrong,* but we may also be less likely to be spiritually engaged. There is a distinct thrill to stumbling upon ancient religious markers, petroglyphs, abandoned mills, or even old war bunkers and letting the imagination run free. It is another thing to arrive at such a site and find it carefully restored and fully interpreted by the anonymous preservation professional: today's Kilroy.

In Britain, preservationists seem less flustered by charges of elitism and less keen on cultural diversity. In the offices of English Heritage and the National Trust, the emphasis is squarely on the architecture, although some consideration has been given to not having preservation occur at the cost of destroying local communities. Preservation in this context has long been considered the preserve of the educated, the genteel, and the upper class. Robert Hewison recounts how Lady Sylvia Sayer described an incident relating to the Dartmoor Preservation Trust, founded by her great-grand-father and grandfather:

> A farming member suggested that the Association should try to recruit more working class people, "not people who read the posh newspapers but the ones who read the *Daily Mirror,* because there are more of them." But a massive local membership is likely to mean the entry of elements that favor unrestricted motoring and caravaning and resent restraints on building or advertising in the National Park. . . . Many local councillors and native Dartmoor inhabitants whose forebears had to fight the moor to wring a living from it are likely to support anything that tames the wilderness, such as more roads, quarries or reservoirs or any other development promising further employment or economic advantage. . . . Dartmoor is unique and of national importance, and can no more be left in the care of local farmers than Oxford's colleges can be left in the care of the car workers of Cowley.[32]

David Lowenthal, having made extensive study of British and American preservation, concurs in the assessment that British preservation is more openly and unconcernedly elitist. Lowenthal writes: "The English National Trust has two million members. But most play no active heritage role. Only a small elite have the requisite expertise and ancestral taste." As an example of the difference, Lowenthal cites an Anglo-American strategy meeting in the early eighties, where British representatives were at first envious of the tax incentives that fueled much of the American preservation effort. "But their treasury and heritage leaders were soon appalled; tax credits would give developers and builders a say in what to save and restore. In Britain these are heritage foes, philistine destroyers. The historic fabric belongs to the Great and the Good; heritage is the pastoral care of **gentlemen**. It was unheard of to open decision making to common commercial folk."[33]

Some British preservationists *would* like to see themselves as spreading a broader preservation net and pulling in properties relating, if not necessarily to ethnic history, then certainly to local and regional history and to working class history. Certainly there has been a major expansion in industrial preservation, as discussed in chapter four. In industrial towns such as Manchester and Leeds, industrial preservation can help rebuild a sense of local pride, even if it cannot restore or substitute for lost jobs.

One new frontier is workers' homes. The National Trust of Scotland has led the way in this, with its preservation of the "little houses" of Fife and the worker row houses of Glasgow. Local boosters want to preserve the Blackpool Tower—long the distinguishing feature of this working class seaside resort—and turn part of its base into an indoor theme park. This, of course, is not exactly the National Trust approach to preservation.

Ethnic diversity is somewhat more difficult than class history to interpret, given that most ethnic communities in Britain are of much more recent origin than are similar communities in the United States. A few cities such as Bradford are discovering that ethnic diversity may mean tourist dollars, especially if it can be promoted in a folklorist, nonthreatening manner.[34] Foods, costumes, and festivals come to the fore more than do structures in efforts to exploit the exotic appeal of Asian and Caribbean cultures.[35]

The very presence of these populations in Britain and of the great ethnic diversity in America suggests that preservationists will have an increasingly difficult job in interpreting culture and history to its publics. As preservation continues to professionalize, it will have to confront serious social issues and become more reflexive about its role in shaping collective memories of groups and nations.

The Social Mapping of Structures and Territory

It is clear that preservation presents different problems in Great Britain than in the United States. A nation with a mere fraction of the land of the latter, Britain's cultural landscape is far more densely packed with prehistoric landworks, Roman and Celtic ruins, ancient Saxon churches, medieval and Tudor houses and inns, great cathedrals, palaces, fortresses, Georgian houses and townscapes, and so on.

The past is a moving point. When preservation began to attract attention in the nineteenth century, the first targets were the old medieval structures: the Gothic was praised and imitated, the Georgian was reviled. After the turn of the century, the tables were turned, spurred by publication of Geoffrey Scott's *The Architecture of Humanism* in 1914.[36] Now the eighteenth-century Georgian country homes were valued as architecture and as history, preparing the way for the Country House Scheme that followed. Today, it is the industrial past and the recent past that are the new targets of preservation.

Such new targets do not replace the old; rather, they are added to them. Thus the "shape of the past" becomes the "weight of the past," as preservation requires an increasing cut of the nation's resources. Within the British National Trust itself, the costs attached to preservation are so great that the Trust will not accept outright gifts of historical and architecturally significant homes unless they come accompanied with a "dowry" of upward of a million pounds.

The United States, by contrast, is a relatively new nation. Underlining this fact, when interest in preserving Indian ruins arose at the turn of the century, it was because they were viewed as providing the missing antiquity: parks such as the Mesa Verde would substitute for Athens and Rome.[37] Periods providing much of the historic lode of Britain—Roman, Saxon, Tudor—were not, in such form, part of American history. Instead, the American Revolution became the major event in the early preservationist narrative, which was extended back to the pilgrims and forward to pioneer settlements across the expanding frontier. Because of this process of historic expansion, what is considered historic in Los Angeles may seem of recent vintage in Boston.

For this reason, the United States has been more willing to plumb the recent past, including the commercial past: early McDonald's hamburger stands are seen as structures worth preserving. Thus, while emphasizing the social-structural and social-psychological elements of preservation, we must also consider the evidence of history. This evidence, however, never stands alone, but requires symbolic interpretation and integration into narratives that convey a greater sense of meaning.

The social mapping of structures occurs across social territories. If Britain early achieved a major centralized organization, it is partly because local elites were more nearly among a unified ruling class than those in America, whose influence was more purely local or at most regional.[38] The British were more closely connected, both socially and territorially, in an age when modern communication and transportation networks were not yet fully achieved. This closer connection clearly facilitated the rapid formation of a national organization, whose interests transcended those of any specific locality.

In choosing major sites for preservation, the British Trust currently takes into account relative distribution across counties. Thus, for example, Wimpole Hall was accepted for preservation not simply because of its evident historic and architectural significance, but also because Cambridgeshire did not have a major country house on the National Trust list. In the United States, similarly, the National Trust operates regional offices and regularly reports on regional activities. As a clearing house, it manages to bind together the once diffuse local efforts through the sharing of information.

▨ *Cultural Consciousness and Cultural Narratives*

Social mapping involves more than the presence of structures distributed over territory. It also involves preservationists' perceptions of their history, its significance, and their own role as its guardians. History, impossible to grasp in its full complexity, is more easily assimilated when placed in the form of cultural narratives. Thus the early British preservationists were influenced by the widely current idea, propagated not just by Burke and Cobbett, but by Coleridge, Ruskin, and Scott, among others, that the Middle Ages were a time characterized by heroic nobility and organic solidarity. They joined others in looking back to this preindustrial "golden age" for inspiration.[39]

In this cultural narrative, the Lake District symbolized, as perhaps no other piece of British landscape, a distilled vision of the preindustrial rural idyll. In this idyll, social relations take their character from the landscape, creating yeoman sturdiness. Hard work and often cruel weather were seen as bringing a special beatitude not to be found in the more modern world to the farmers and their families. It appeared both natural and right that when the railroad, the harbinger of the industrial order, threatened to cut right through this sacred vale, social activists joined together in its defense. The golden-age image is further and more widely reinforced through the magnificent country homes and their surrounding parks and landscape, which give an impression of both social and natural harmony.

In the United States, early preservationists helped write cultural narratives for a people without king or crown. The early emphasis on patriotic sites must be seen as part of a wider, mid-nineteenth-century fascination with the nation's founding. Some of this fervor can be traced to the political convulsions of the pre– and post–Civil War period, to the effort to recapture, or, more accurately, reaffirm the presumed unity of the early days of nationhood. Some of it derives from the changing socioeconomic order, as new immigrants arrived and had to be assimilated. Older arrivals themselves were being drawn from rural villages and towns to the expanding cities and toward the frontier, while the quality of life also changed dramatically for those who remained in the small towns and villages of the Eastern seaboard. For all these reasons, the American narratives took on a pointedly patriotic, didactic form directed more toward inculcating political virtue than toward encouraging aesthetic appreciation.

The second wave of American preservation also reflected underlying structural dislocations. Historians have described the period surrounding the turn of the century as a great transition, during which American society moved from one set of values, associated primarily with local, rural communities (for example, religion, kinship, tradition) to those values associated with modern urban society (business competitiveness, social and geographic mobility, an emphasis on innovation and social change). A transition of such magnitude made for a dramatic saga that communicated to the nation a sense of purpose and destiny. Preservation provided settings in which portions of this saga could be ritualistically reenacted. These presentations confirmed the inevitableness of the path from past to present as they reaffirmed the superiority of capitalism, progress, and the American way of life.

Thus, historic preservation reflects the new class alignments that resulted from industrialization. In Britain, the social role of preservation activists was twofold, a contradictory response to the new status disjunctions. On the one hand, the depth of class consciousness gave rise to efforts to create new bases of communal harmony and of national identification. On the other, these same efforts may, as Dellheim suggests, "have reinforced the hegemony of local elites, who assumed the roles of proprietors of the past as well as masters of the present."[40] The social role of symbolic banker effectively merged both purposes.

When a preexisting traditional order is undermined by the forces of industrialization, new forms of social organization, such as clubs and voluntary associations, move into the void to create a new basis for community activity and identification.[41] Perhaps, in their interest in preservation, archaeology, antiquities, and natural history, these Victorians were searching for a new base for social relations in communities where the earlier order had been undermined by industrialization and the new class structure.

But preservation was not simply a case of rich vs. poor, upper class versus new working class. Instead, interest in preservation was shared by two major status groups. Social elites looked back to the past to legitimate their present power and to maintain it in this new context, while culturally progressive forces, an identifiable status group of artists and intellectuals, saw in preservation an alternative to the human and natural costs of industrialization. Each group opposed the new industrial bourgeoisie, whose enterprises were destroying both the traditional countryside and the traditional social hierarchy.[42] Thus the past can be made to serve a range of political purposes even as it gives rise to identifiable "taste cultures."[43]

The very idea of the National "Trust" reflects a tutorial relationship established between preservationists and the populace, a relationship of unequals, as between teacher and student.[44] Through the authority of the Trust, preservationists were self-appointed custodians of a national legacy until such time as all others shared their particular appreciation of Britain's past. As Fedden writes, "In a Utopia where a perfect sense of values prevailed there would be no place for a National Trust."[45] Yet the very idea of "perfect values" supports the criticism of elites who pretend that their interpretations are the only correct interpretations. This confounds the social with the natural and results in "symbolic violence" committed against other classes who would reasonably and rightly hold different interpretations.[46]

In the United States, preservation initially served as one means of social integration: not just of classes but, equally important, of the increasingly diverse racial and ethnic populations. The homes of local heroes, revolutionary leaders, and of presidents were meant to teach civic obedience both to new generations and to new immigrants arriving through the nineteenth and early twentieth centuries. They helped construct civic identities. Joshua Taylor has described how the idea of the "American" was early layered with distinctive regional colorings.[47] At the same time, however, patriotic icons, chief among them George Washington, spanned these regions and signified to Americans that, despite their differences, they really were all one nation.[48]

At the regional level, it is interesting that the society that most resembles the British organization is the SPNEA, founded in 1910. The class position of the Boston Brahmins and intellectuals most clearly approximated that of their British counterparts. Their assumption of responsibility for the tradition embedded within this region most resembles this particular "tradition of service" among the early British philanthropists. Other regions developed their own organizations, methods, and goals.

This localistic and regional emphasis within American preservation reflects pluralism in the social structure and in its ideology. Volunteerism is also part of this ideology. French sociologist Hervé Varenne has remarked on how small-town Americans feel they must always be constructing society anew through voluntary activity.[49] Varenne is reiterating a point first made by de Tocqueville about the American obsession with volunteerism and participation. Preservation has very much this quality in America and draws upon these strengths.

Back to Utopia ▨ CHAPTER 3

To fully enjoy and appreciate your visit to Old Bethpage, try to imagine yourself living in this farm community of the 1800's. Stroll leisurely and let the serene tranquility surround you. . . . Let the mood of the village engulf you as you stand quietly on a hillock— listen for the faint ring of the blacksmith's anvil, the church bells, the rattle of horse- drawn wagons.
—*Old Bethpage Enquirer and Long Island Advertiser*

Where is utopia? Modernists hoped to find it in the future. Science was supposed to create a brave new world where technology solved every problem and resolved every social tension. Socialism also provided utopian visions of a different sort. Followers hoped it would lead inevitably toward its goal of the perfect socialist state, the end point and ultimate resolution of history's long saga of class conflict.[1]

While modernists located utopia in the future, it has just as frequently been located somewhere in the past. Arcady was the classical utopia, a soft land radiant with beauty. Many societies look back on their own mythical golden age. Different strains of primitivistic philosophy argue for the natural superiority of other times and places. Sometimes, utopia was a hard place that brought out natural virtues: Sparta, as it was viewed from the safe distance of the

Renaissance, is one example. Sometimes it was a land of milk and honey: the peasant's Cockaigne.[2]

Certain historic representations are, in fact, representations not of a preexisting historic reality, but of a mythical utopia situated somewhere in the past. For purposes of analysis, these representations can be called "Staged Symbolic Communities" (SSCs).[3] Staged Symbolic Communities are representations of past communities, whether reconstructed on an original site, such as Colonial Williamsburg, Virginia, or imaginative recreations of generic communities without specific historic referent. For example, at Old Sturbridge Village in southeastern Massachusetts, historic buildings were gathered from all over New England and placed in a locality where no previous village had existed. SSCs can also exist alongside so-called "living communities," as is the case in Amana, Iowa, a former German communal society. There, some buildings have been given over to the interpretation of the past and others remain private, serving the needs of present residents.[4]

All communities manipulate symbols to define their boundaries and identity. These preserved or re-created villages are *themselves* symbols: they perform community in a society where organic communities are a thing of the past, if, indeed, they ever existed. Ralf Dahrendorf's insights into utopia and society will help demonstrate how these villages play this symbolic role and point out some of the important social issues involved in the portrayal.

▧ Community and Utopia

For Dahrendorf, what all utopias from Plato's Republic onward share is the *absence of change.* Whether Orwellian nightmare or romantic dream, utopias stand strangely apart from historic processes. Utopias have certain structural prerequisites. As Dahrendorf writes, "It is no accident that the catchwords of Huxley's Brave New World—'Community, Identity, Stability'—can be applied with equal justice to most other utopias."[5]

If lack of historic process is a first distinguishing characteristic of utopias, Dahrendorf argues that a second characteristic is the utopic community's seemingly *universal consensus* regarding social values and institutions. This consensus can be enforced, as in Orwell's *1984*. Or it can arise naturally, as a form of social contract based on the General Will of the citizenry. Whether consensus is natural or enforced, the result is that conflict is absent. As Dahrendorf writes, "Utopian societies may be and indeed often are caste societies; but they are not class societies in which the oppressed revolt against their oppressors."[6] The resulting social harmony is one of the sources of the apparent social stability.

At the same time as presenting an image of harmony and stability, utopias must also incorporate some form of activity. They cannot simply exist. As a third characteristic, the processes that occur in utopian societies are *recurrent and cyclical*. They do not upset the established way of life; rather, they sustain it. The division of labor is the "metabolism of society" and serves to uphold the status quo.

A final and fourth characteristic is the fact that utopias appear to stand *isolated from other communities*. This isolation is not just in time but in space. Utopias are notable for how they differ from the rest of the world. They "are monolithic and homogenous communities, suspended not only in time but also in space, shut off from the outside world, which might, after all, present a threat to the cherished immobility of the social structure."[7] Let us now examine how these four characteristics of utopias are present in Staged Symbolic Communities.

▨ *Staged Symbolic Communities as Utopias*

Ahistoricity. While they purport to represent history, Staged Symbolic Communities stand curiously located out of time. Curators may have a specific date or decade that they aim to represent. Sturbridge Village is set at 1830; Blists Hill, a staged industrial village in England's Ironbridge Gorge, is set for the 1880s–1890s. But the visitor sees a community fixed "somewhere in the past," caught in time, because there is nothing pushing it into the present.

Villagers go about their business happily, gaily even, totally ignorant of the forces of change. The only "time" such communities recognize is repetitive, seasonal change. Time moves on without progressing. The discontinuity between present and past, and the consequent denial of future possibilities, also means that the social processes most community sociologists see as central to the life of real communities are simply nonexistent. Any social, political, or economic issues such as may arise in this bizarre context are decided not by historic "residents," but by contemporary curators and officials.

SSCs also represent a break with history insofar as they themselves were at some point created, or re-created. Time did not stand still in Williamsburg. It jumped backwards. There was a small and economically depressed community extant at Williamsburg in the early 1920s, when a local minister, William A. R. Goodwin, began researching into the history of the site. He became increasingly aware of the potential in its remaining historic structures, then hidden behind false shop fronts, gas pumps, and tacked-on advertisements. Goodwin contacted John D. Rockefeller, whom he convinced that Williamsburg represented a golden opportunity to resurrect the past.

It was a particular vision of the past that appealed to Rockefeller. Even as his own companies, such as Standard Oil, were helping destroy the historic fabric of many ongoing communities with new roads and gas stations to serve the automobile age, he helped reconstruct the golden image of a mythical Georgian past, which itself harkened back to earlier images of classical perfection. This image, translated into "Colonial Williamsburg" sur-reality, destroyed the actual, ongoing history of the real Williamsburg community, which was quite literally sold out from under its residents. These residents, a sizable proportion of whom were black or poor white, were no match for the Rockefeller millions. As this historic community was dismantled and its residents dispersed, an ahistoric Staged Symbolic Community was created in its place.

In founding Greenfield Village, Henry Ford collected historic buildings from far and wide: Edison's laboratories from New Jersey, a Cotswold cottage, a Scottish schoolhouse. Ford's stated motive was to show that history, in some sense, was all wrong—at least the official version that appeared in textbooks. That history, in his famous line, was "bunk." Greenfield Village was, like all mythic creations, designed to be "realer than real." As total fabrication and historic pastiche, it was designed to communicate mythic truths concerning America's greatness and the inexorable path of progress. It was what historian Thomas Schlereth calls a "middle landscape," whose purpose was both pedagogy and moral uplift.[8]

The founder of Old Sturbridge Village was Albert O. Wells, head of American Optical Company in Southbridge, Massachusetts. As Wells's father had been a farmer, he felt himself rooted to New England, even as his own work formed part of its industrial transformation. Wells had a particular appreciation for old tools; during the depression families would come from miles to sell him their "junk." His son, who had studied John Dewey's pragmatic philosophy at school, advised his father on the importance of learning by doing. He suggested that Wells' collection of tools might be best displayed in a small village, where visitors could observe the replicated activities of the nineteenth-century farmers and craftsmen.[9] The end goal was "To preserve the ever-good things of New England's past in a manner that will teach their usefulness to the people of the present and the future . . . above all, how virtues and ideals expressed in them can be applied to life and work today."[10] This was the explicit pedagogic purpose behind Wells's new historic village.

One can speculate as to why these leading industrialists found it attractive to re-create images of preindustrial America. A similar phenomenon did not occur in Great Britain at the same time or to the same extent. One explanation would be that in Britain, "fake villages" would receive stiff competition from real villages. Interestingly, the most famous "fake village," Portmeirion in north Wales, is a village of total individual fancy without pretense to historic reality.

I would suggest that American millionaires, in contrast to their British counterparts, felt the subjective need to create the village that would complement their new "lord of the manor" status. In Britain, the village comes with the territory and the title. Or, at least, it used to.[11]

The one exception in Britain proves the rule, insofar as it was created not by a British lord but an American millionaire. In 1903 William Waldorf Astor bought Hever Castle. As part of its restoration, he created an adjoining "Tudor Village," in part because the old moated castle was too small for his lavish entertainments and lifestyle. Varying facades of brick, sandstone, plasterwork, and half-timbering give the impression of individual cottages that have been built up slowly and altered by time. This impression is belied by internal corridors that connect the over one hundred rooms that served Astor as guest rooms, estate offices, and servants quarters. Today, this early twentieth-century Tudor Village is a Grade I Listed Building, meaning it is considered highly deserving of conservation and subject to the greatest measure of controls. It is also available for corporate and private functions. A brochure describes it as "particularly appropriate for companies whose executives want to get away together for a few days in conditions of high comfort and security." Astor, a consummate capitalist, no doubt would have approved.

Social Consensus. Social order implies a moral order. One of the reasons these villages are popular tourist attractions is that they are so pleasant and agreeable. Everyone appears to share in a common contentment as they greet visitors or go about their business.[12] SSCs present the basis of their moral order in religion, which is demonstrated visually by the prominent place they assign the tall white church in the village plan. The only evidence of enforced consensus is the stocks, which are not meant to be taken seriously, but rather serve as an amusing prop for family photographs. Otherwise, all villagers appear to be motivated by a General Will to subjugate individual desire to the common good. In fact, they appear to be strangely lacking in desire, like Stepford Wives removed to another time and place.

As Freud aptly remarked, morality often entails high standards of cleanliness.[13] SSCs are clean beyond reason and out-of-keeping with historic reality. They also don't smell bad. The stench that would have permeated a whaling town like Mystic is totally absent from the staged reconstruction. The pollution that was an ever present fact in industrial towns is also lacking in Ironbridge Gorge.

Both landscape *and* inhabitants, then, are clean, innocent, and unspoiled. An advertisement draws the reader in with a silhouetted Amish farmer and his mule team: "Spring in Pennsylvania Dutch Country. Uncrowded, Unhurried, & Almost Perfect." The copy continues, "The fields turn the brightest, freshest shade of green, Amish farmers plant with mule drawn equipment, Spring flowers and orchards bloom."

SSCs celebrate their moral order in rituals meant to demonstrate rural or ethnic values. Staged events offer an image of ethnic authenticity which may or may not be grounded in historic reality. Indian dances are presented out of their social and religious context in sites across the Southwest. The Amana Colonies host Oktoberfests quite at odds with their sober, pietist background and with their earlier admonition to "shun Outsiders." Such "pseudo-events" have all the advantages of planning.[14] They are pleasurable, colorful, and offer plentiful opportunities for consumption and photography.

Much of the appeal of SSCs is that they promise and deliver two social goods that are usually seen as contradictory. They offer new experience, and they promise security. It is their ability to deliver both that makes them safe bets for two sizable social categories, namely senior citizens and school children. This subjective experience of history is designed to be "fun for the whole family," meaning it is *safe* for the whole family. Sex and violence are usually, incongruously, absent from SSCs. When depicted, as in characters such as frontier town madams and events such as cowboy shootouts, they provide more color than conflict: a titillating new experience that does not threaten one's security.

Thus part of the nostalgic vision of an innocent past is the vision of the pre-Freudian family: safe from both external threats *and* internal conflicts. Wherever possible, SSCs present an exhibit meant to depict a typical family home of a pioneer or Amish family, etc. Even in the Amana Colonies, where people lived in multifamily houses, the Amana *Heim* (Home) Museum seems laid out for a nuclear family. Such exhibits gloss over how many town residents were single, widowed, divorced, or separated, and how many children were left orphaned.

Repetitive Activity. While visiting historic villages is meant to be a leisure experience, a large component of what tourists actually see are what Dean MacCannell has called "work displays." As MacCannell writes, "Modernity is transforming labor into cultural productions attended by tourists and sightseers who are moved by the universality of work relations—*not* as this is represented through their own work (from which they are alienated), but as it is revealed to them at their leisure through the displayed work of others."[15]

The work that is depicted is utopian as it appears to arise naturally out of the interaction between people and their environment. Each task and chore makes sense in itself while also contributing to the greater scheme of things: the productive power of the community. As MacCannell notes, work displays are open, in the sense of open to public view. They appear natural and good, for it is evident the workers have nothing to hide. Work sites are cleaned up, no trash or objectionable items, and workers themselves are cleaned up, tidy in dress, polite and cooperative.[16]

While historic modes of production are enacted in work displays, modern work is kept behind the scenes or underemphasized. Curators and fund raisers, cleaning crews and maintenance men are not meant to be the object of tourist attention, but rather merely facilitate the tourist's appreciation and understanding of the historic work displays. These modern forms of work, both bureaucratic and physical, become the invisible hand that keeps the village turning over, if not progressing.

As Dahrendorf noted of utopias, workers in these historic displays appear locked into preindustrial caste positions and content in them. Even representations that enact later periods often present social class as a given, not a problem. One striking example is provided in the summer cottages of Newport, Rhode Island, a stage set from the period and the people who inspired Veblen's analysis of the leisure class.[17]

Throughout the tours of these cottages, tourists are encouraged to identify with the ruling class and to find the servants amusing. At Biltmore, perhaps the most magnificent of the "cottages," a dramatic troupe enacts an *Upstairs Downstairs* social-class charade. The upstairs characters include Miss Whitfield of Brighton, England ("a rebellious debutante"); Captain Horatio Rumprear of the British Royal Navy; Miss Ruth Twombly of new Jersey ("a socialite with a notorious taste for the risqué"); and Trevor Ashley Doddington III (yachtsman, polo player, philanthropist, "known to be flirtatious but not a scoundrel"). Downstairs characters include James Peabody, seventh serving man (who left London with hopes of making it in the Colonies); Winifred Crump, fourth housemaid (shy but eager and hardworking); Jonathan John Weathermore, fourth serving man (whose "irrepressible sense of humor often gets him in trouble"); and Daphne Entwhistle (raised in London, who "still retains her Cockney accent and sense of humor"). Weathermore and Entwhistle would need more than a sense of humor to bear up under the demands that were placed on the servant class and that made most people flee it as soon as any alternatives, including factory work, were present. But the severity of domestic service is rarely stressed in historic houses, where the interpretation focuses on the owner's family history, achievements, and artifacts. Often the servants' quarters are not open for public view. Ironically, sometimes they become the space appropriated for preservationists' offices and/or curators' private quarters.

If such nostalgic representations are fun for the whole family, they are also meant to be educational. Both adults and children dutifully set about learning lessons about the past, as long as they're not too difficult or demanding. Visitors do the "work" of tourism as they follow the designated trail through the villages and as they watch exhibits and demonstrations.

A curious process of role playing commences as the visitor begins to interact with "interpreters"—the temporary-but-pretend-permanent residents of historic villages. This results in an intriguing contradiction. In the first instance, visitors revert to the status of child in a tutorial relationship.[18] They stand quietly, respectfully, as interpreters go through their presentations. Some of the better tourist-students prepare questions, which they hope to get the chance to ask. The teachers, the interpreters, have adult status insofar as they have *knowledge* of preindustrial or early industrial work processes.

On a deeper level, however, the parent-child roles are reversed, hence the contradiction. Tourists know that the knowledge being delivered is no knowledge at all: unnecessary, outmoded, anachronistic. In this sense, they know more than the interpreters. Visitors play the adult role because they represent adult society—the sophisticated, knowing capitalist society that developed out of these *innocent* beginnings. A spokesman for Mystic said the community "brings people back to a more innocent era." Interpreters work together harmoniously at their set tasks, knowing that by serving the common good they serve their own interests. Visitors know that the skills depicted are of little or no value in the real marketplace outside the village representation.

There is more to the superior position of the visitor's knowledge, which transcends the communal setting, and the interpreter's, which is particular to it. There is, after all, a story being enacted, and the tourist experiences the pleasures of the narrative.[19] Like readers of popular romances, tourists know the familiar plot and take comfort in it.[20] There's a titillating pleasure in knowing more than the characters, whether they're in a book or standing in front of you, real as life. SSCs have begun to realize the psychic play afforded and have begun to provide "naive" characters. As one example, a colonial seaman just returned to Mystic encounters two visiting English tourists, one of whom tells him she's English. He responds, "But so am I Madame! So are we all!"

The plot in these narratives is seldom explicit, but then, it is not supposed to be. As Lyotard remarks, narrative is not history but the opposite of history.[21] Narrative takes the raw material of history and alters it to make a better story. The visitor is lulled back into childhood and does not have to take responsibility for understanding the past, much less the complexities and strange twists on the road to the present.

Thus nostalgic representations offer a range of experiences. While visitors perform the work of tourism, it is at a leisurely pace, and far more restful than the work reenacted in the sawmill. In addition, visitors satisfy what Freud called their "libido for looking" as they see displays far different from their usual surroundings. When they tire of visual and cognitive pleasures, tourists can indulge in oral pleasures. It is no accident that inns, restaurants, candy stores and snack bars figure prominently in village layouts, and, in terms of traffic, prove some of their most popular attractions.

Besides consuming Colonial popovers and German sauer-braten, visitors are, more importantly, consuming history. Staged Symbolic Communities are like the factory outlet villages that spring up in their vicinity. They offer lots of history crowded into a relatively small area. All have shops either within or immediately outside the community, where visitors are encouraged to buy souvenirs —some specific to the site, others included because they suggest Americana or a nostalgic approach to domesticity. In some instances, the line between the historic village and consumer villages is so blurred that visitors no longer recognize the difference. Interstate 80 has an exit stop in eastern Iowa called Little Amana, where the tourist shops, restaurants, and motels have frequently been mistaken for the real Amana villages located several miles off the road. Advertisements for Pennsylvania Dutch country further blur the distinction. On the same page as an advertisement for "the Amish Village," with its blacksmith shop, one-room school, and guided Amish house tours, another advertisement for "the Village that has it all" invites tourists to "*sleep* in spacious guest rooms, *dine* in their restaurant and *shop* in over 80 factory outlets." Neither "village" bears much resemblance to a real Amish village, kept backstage to most tourists. The emphasis on pre- and early-industrial produc-tion inside the village is mirrored by the postmodern consumerism outside.

Isolation. Staged Symbolic Communities are clearly delim-ited spatially. It is evident when one is entering or leaving the community. This may be accomplished simply through discreet signs marking village borders or through billboards welcoming the visi-tor to the community. Borders may also be tightly monitored by the use of high fences and admissions booths. A *zone of mediation* is thus established to facilitate and exploit the transition between out-side world and utopian community. At Sturbridge, this zone includes the vast parking field, the entrance, and visitor center, which col-lects the entrance fees and directs tourists as to the correct way to "see" community, both logistically and imaginatively. On the way out, tourists stop in, as if required, at the large gift shop, where they purchase Sturbridge souvenirs and other objects with links, however tenuous, to early America. While inside, visitors discover a village that is human scale. In contrast to suburban sprawl and overgrown urban areas, SSCs can be taken in and walked through in one experience. The layout is well organized, frequently with buildings arranged along a village green, with several small tourist trails meandering off. Automobile traffic is usually outlawed. Sheep safely graze. First impressions are reassuring.

Just as the space is organized in SCCs, so it time manipulated. As they pass through village gates, tourists travel back, as a Sturbridge pamphlet puts it, "to see up close how life in New England used to be, in the days when most families still earned their living from tilling the soil, when picturesque villages were just beginning to dot the landscape, and when strong individuals like Emerson, Thoreau, and Daniel Webster seemed to stand as tall as New England's rugged hills."

This need to control both time and space is especially difficult to satisfy in living communities, where the present always threatens to intrude upon the past. There is increased consciousness of the need to preserve not just historic buildings, but the surrounding views in historic communities such as Waterford, Virginia, and Historic Deerfield, Massachusetts.[22] Within these communities, specific strategies must be developed to negotiate the desires of tourists to penetrate into community and to share its authentic experiences, and the desires of the community to protect some of its social processes from public view.[23] These strategies manipulate space and time by creating areas, activities, and periods that are off-limits.

Collective action may take the form of an overall charge to tourists on behalf of the community and severe restriction of front-stage social action.[24] Such is the case in Taos, New Mexico, where the steady stream of tourists are charged a hefty entrance fee, plus a fee for each camera they intend to use (which is then tagged). In addition, they are instructed not to photograph any of the residents without asking specific permission, and possibly rewarding them for their cooperation. Much of the tourist activity is confined to the central area where cars are parked and from which tourists can view the architecture of this settlement and also gain access to the historic church. Residents stare silently out at the tourists, who quickly get the message that wandering in the back regions is discouraged.

In the Amanas, descendants of the original German pietist communards must negotiate their needs with the needs of tourists, who support many of the community's businesses. Here confinement of the tourists to a front-stage arena is more difficult, insofar as historic sites and tourist-oriented businesses are scattered throughout the seven villages on their twenty-five thousand-acre tract. Tourists often make a point of at least driving through each of the seven villages, collecting them as though they were different national parks. Tour maps and an extensive signage system attempt to keep the tourists on approved tracks, but some tourists wander off either in ignorance or in pursuit of the authentic. Some forget that most Amana homes are private property, rather than museums or services. Residents report tourists picnicking on front lawns or even walking into houses to ask when dinner will be served.[25]

In SSCs with defensible boundaries, tourism may be restricted to specific hours. Given the extensiveness and dispersion of Amana attractions, this delimitation is more difficult to achieve. Amana residents adjust their activities to the tourist ebb and flow. They make intensive use of the early hours to do gardening and any local shopping. They also emphasize how the community "returns to them" in the evening and in the less hectic off-season.

Other strategies available for managing tourism include maintaining a sharp psychic divide between insiders and outsiders and fleeing the community during the tourist season, becoming tourists themselves in search of the authentic elsewhere. Amana people who remain in the villages report a sense of unease when asked to perform, as if they were part of a living exhibit. One resident fought back by wearing a tee shirt proclaiming, "I'm not a tourist, I live here!" At Taos, some Indian boys express their annoyance by throwing pebbles at tourists.

Taos and Amana both represent ethnic communities where

tourist penetration has necessitated considerable interpretation and regulation. By contrast, in other historic communities minimalist strategies are used. Litchfield, Connecticut, presents a genteel facade that is historically inaccurate but visually appealing to contemporary tastes.[26] Stately white structures with dark shutters sit proudly on streets that radiate from the village green. These houses are not, however, open to the public, nor does the public expect them to be. Interpretive acts are limited to performances in the museum and school, and consumer services are contained in a few shops and restaurants facing the green.

Historic Deerfield, like Litchfield, does not advertise extensively. Contrasting itself to Old Sturbridge Village, with its busloads of tourists, Historic Deerfield seeks to attract the "right sort of tourist," usually middle to upper class and with a specific interest in early American architecture and crafts. Historic Deerfield has a village store and an up-market inn.

In sharp contrast to the restraint exercised in these two Anglo-American communities, it may be argued that an attitude associated with processes of internal colonialism affects historic communities of diverse ethnic or racial origins. Like colonized people, these ethnic groups are considered as somewhat backward, and thereby exotic or charming for visitors. Tourists expect to see folkloric presentations of dance and song and to view residents in their historic costumes rather than modern dress. Visitors express disappointment that Amana residents no longer wear the heavy, dark clothing now associated with the Amish and when Indian youths ride mopeds rather than stallions. Such folkloric displays are not expected of the upper class who own the Litchfield houses or the privileged students of the Deerfield Academy. For them, historic dress is strictly optional.

Community, Utopia, and Ideology

Thus, Staged Symbolic Communities differ from "real communities" in evident and important ways. Their "residents" often don't permanently reside there, nor simply perform social roles, but rather interpret historic social roles to tourists. SSCs are also, as we have seen, located out of historic time and exist without the social processes that define authentic community interaction.

While Sturbridge, for example, would not be recognized as a "real" community, many that might be so considered fail to live up to sociological definitions and expectations of community. For Herbert Gans, the prototypical planned postwar community, Levittown, was not a "real" community as he defined it. "It was not an economic unit whose members were dependent on each other for their livelihood, and it was not a social unit for there was no reason or incentive for people to relate to each other as Levittowners on any regular or recurring basis. And Levittown was clearly not a symbolic unit, for the sense of community was weak."[27] If it wasn't a community, what then was it? Gans suggests it could best be considered "an administrative-political unit that encompassed an aggregate of community-wide associations within a pre-defined space."[28]

What was true of Levittown is increasingly true for other communities. Today, planned communities, whether suburban developments or urban condominiums, are organized around "concepts" and offer desirable leisure facilities. Many, however, lack the integrating economic and social ties, which Gans uses as criteria of community. Older, once "organic" communities also become economic shells, as women, formerly overrepresented among those doing the "work" of community increasingly look for work outside the community, and as corporations and professions demand ever more of the energies of both men and women.[29]

The irony, then, is that while SSCs are not real communities by sociological standards, however slack or rigorous, to many tourist visitors they seem *more* like real communities than do their home localities.[30] This paradox is central to our understanding of Staged Symbolic Communities. SSCs are an increasingly significant feature of our social landscape, in part because they present images of coherent, organic communities: they are small towns and villages whose secure boundaries selectively filter the impact of the greater society, rather than being overcome by it.

Thus, while SSCs present images of utopia, they also serve an ideological purpose in modern society. SSCs are exemplars providing

lessons in the "good community"; whether fake or real is of no concern in the age of facadism. These lessons can be summarized as
follows:

The good community is the genteel community. It is clean and
harmonious; residents share the same refined tastes. This was the
image provided by Williamsburg, the "Williamsburg look" that
added fuel to the ongoing Colonial Revival.[31] This genteel image has
been adopted as a model for up-market communities and even down-
market condominiums. Rockefeller's upper-class gentility becomes
translated into middle-class conformity. Houses are painted in
either white, as in Litchfield's uniform facades, or in approved
colonial colors: Pilgrim Red, Newport Gray, Tavern Green.

The good community is the protected community. To enter an
SSC the visitor passes through a gatehouse, for such ideal communities could not exist in the middle of suburban sprawl without
some form of symbolic divide. Gatehouses are now an important
architectural feature of new communities being built. They are an
important part of the new definition of marketable communities,
insofar as they offer both the appearance of social status and the
illusion of security.

The good community is conflict free. One does not see SSC
residents at odds over new development plans or prospective neigh-
bors. The behavior of SSC residents, like every other aspect of life,
is, in fact, governed by management. The management is not seen,
but it makes rules that even tourists are required to obey: keep to
the paths, no defacing of property, no professional photography without permission.

Like SSCs, the governing boards of private communities and
condominiums draw up lists of rules that prohibit the unsightly and
the unseemly: speed limits of thirty miles an hour, no parking
along the streets, no dogs off the leash, no wash hanging on balconies,
no broken-down cars in carports. Many potential sources of conflict are thereby ruled out ahead of time. Residents themselves can
be expected to play their social roles within these strictures more
consciously and conscientiously, like the "residents" of SSCs. Their
expressed values and behavior must conform to an ever more
tightly drawn, class-specific set of rules and norms. In Mystic, a local

historian emphasizes the residents' "great consciousness in maintaining the place of these homes in history." The result is to guarantee both the personal and the financial investment in history.

Personal and social history can be rewritten. A critical part
of Freud's vision was that people were shaped by their personal histories: histories could not be unwritten or changed, but only
revealed and dealt with rationally. The "history of nations" was also
long held to set a course which each nation followed. One studied
history both for a sense of the past and a sobering balance to the
events of the present. History provided an anchor against the consuming whirlpool of political events and mass enthusiasms.[32]

History, however, has been sucked into a whirlpool. It is not
treated as past actuality, but as present possibility—raw material
to be shaped by contemporary exigencies. Nietzsche was overcome by the weight of history; modern social actors simply dismantle
history and reassemble it in whatever piece of *bricolage* they
fancy.

This manipulation applies to individual history and also to the
fraudulent assumption of aristocratic identities through fashions and
other status props. It also applies to group and even national history.
The attempt to write the holocaust out of history is notorious, but
there are other acts of omission relating to Samoa, to Watergate,
and on down to the community level.[33]

In the process, many nostalgic representations recall Marx's
dictum that history repeats itself, the first time as tragedy, the
second time as farce. The Middle Ages were a time of periodic
want and suffering for a large percentage of the population. Now this
historic period is gaily reenacted, both in England, in early Tudor
castles, and even more farcically, in America, which clearly did not
participate in the European Middle Ages. Nonetheless, medieval
theme parks promise a "return to the days of chivalry, knight-
hood and honor . . . as a guest of a regal Count & Countess inside
a completely enclosed, air conditioned, European-style Castle." A
medieval festival is even incongruously included as part of the
Amish country schedule of pseudo-events.

*The smart locality is one that either exploits old history, or
creates new history.* History, as we have seen, becomes a product

to be consumed. In Amana, local history was considered by some residents to be like "the goose that laid the golden eggs." The major concern was that the goose should continue laying golden eggs: in other words, the tourist potential should be properly exploited to avoid overexposure and a decline in the quality of the tourist's encounter with history, as carefully manipulated and presented by the community.[34]

In the nineteenth century, communities competed to become stops on the railroad line and to attract industry. In the late twentieth century, communities compete to become stops on the tourist trail and to attract the service industries that feed on tourism. New frontier towns are created across the West, as local boosters climb on board this new train to wealth and opportunity.[35]

In the process, the line between fake and real becomes blurred. Often, ironically, whatever authentic community identity exists gets destroyed in the process, as in the small Catskill communities bracing themselves for the arrival of ParcEurope. Under the development plans, "authentic European villages" (along with Robin Hood and an equestrian school) would replace authentic rural American villages. While many residents opposed the plans, one welcomed the idea, saying it would be like "having Europe in my backyard. . . . I can walk there. I won't even have to fight the traffic or the airlines."[36] ParcEurope, then, promised to be more amusing than either rural New York or Europe and without the hassles of modern society.

In Europe itself, the tension between old and new models of community is pervasive. Olde England and modern England coexist with some difficulty. The tension between the two images and forms of social organizations is reflected in different visions and goals. One manifestation was the battle between Prince Charles and the architects. This was not simply a debate over architectural style. Rather, it reflected profound differences in how the social actors believed society should be organized. Charles's vision was both nostalgic and organic: it was successful on a small scale, as in community architecture, but less keyed into the exigencies of large-scale urban planning.

Utopias serve ideological purposes, but they can also be a form of social critique, presenting alternative solutions. Visitors to Staged

Symbolic Communities take away more than souvenirs and decorating ideas. They also come away with lessons regarding identity, history, and community. The "Williamsburg effect" involves more than paint colors and the attractive presentation of historic villages. It is now the leading architectural model for new communities, the colonial town replacing suburban sprawl.[37] We have yet to see whether this model will prove that contemporary interpretations of past traditions can create radical change, resulting in the restoration of community structure and affective ties.[38] Or these nostalgic villages may remain what they presently appear, a time out from modern society, a step back into utopia.

The
Interpretation
of Industrial
Society

CHAPTER 4

> *Relive the past at the Gladstone Pottery Museum . . .*
> *Go underground. Discover mining through the centuries at Chatterley Whitfield Coal Mining Museum . . .*
> *Discover the rich industrial heritage at Cheddleton Flint Mill and the steam railway at Foxfield . . .*
> —Staffordshire County Council
> tourist brochure, England

Scholars debate whether or not America and Britain are now postindustrial societies or merely late industrial societies.[1] But all agree that the heyday of traditional, productive industry is past. Like earlier historic periods, industrial society becomes the subject of social interpretation. Artifacts from beam engines to early sewing machines become objects with both inherent material qualities and a role to play in newly written historical narratives. These historic narratives not only tell people a version of who they once were, but who they are now, and whether it was worth the trip. Such interpretations thus have an obvious ideological function in linking past to present.

Historians and sociologists have proposed that technology is socially constructed, rather than simply following its own internal logic and imperative.[2] But if technology is socially constructed, it is also socially *reconstructed* through historic preservation and interpretation.

Industrial preservation is relatively new. Compared to the preservation of traditional, agrarian society, it has several obvious drawbacks. Industrialization was a dirty, smelly, dangerous affair. It also presents a complicated story, with international linkages and flows of raw materials being processed into finished goods. We are still divided as to the end of its story, whether or not industrialization was an overall curse or blessing to humankind.

What industrial preservation shares with other forms of preservation, however, is its openness to interpretation. Through the course of history, industrial objects and structures are decontextualized and recontextualized. The preservation process elaborates upon and further defines this process of change, which also affords opportunities for meditation on humanity and the machine.

Industrial Recontextualizations: Forms

An industrial object is defined as any identifiable item produced by industrial society. It can have aided in production (cotton gin, coal mines) or have been a new form of consumption of goods (tinned food) or leisure object (steam-powered boats and carrousels). It can also have represented new social and service improvements (vaccinations, Victorian plumbing). Large objects are considered "structures" and include collieries, mills, and railways.

It is difficult to locate the beginning and end of industrial society, if, indeed, it has ended. Some scholars distinguish a period of early industrial organization in the sixteenth and seventeenth centuries, when advances in areas as diverse as transportation, milling, and mining laid the groundwork for the great industrial expansion in the eighteenth and nineteenth centuries. Other scholars emphasize that the concern to preserve and interpret the productive breakthroughs of the industrial heyday must be extended forward to the myriad consumer goods of the twentieth century.[3]

As with other forms of preservation, the strategies are opportunistic, using what appears in good condition or is donated, and searching for the right object to complete the historic narrative. What use this group of "symbolic bankers" makes of the symbolic capital depends upon the material qualities of the objects themselves, including size (a mining shaft offers different possibilities than a medicine chest); the social role of the bankers (his/her class position, training, and affiliation); and also the manifest and latent social purposes behind the activity (profit or nonprofit, education and/or entertainment). Furthermore, all these considerations affect how industrial objects are presented. The following represent major forms of recontextualization.

The Isolated Object

The German word for monument, *Denkmal,* may be translated as "occasion for reflection." Victorians took the monuments of an earlier period, ruined abbeys and monasteries, as settings for both recreation and reflection. Sites such as Fountains Abbey in Yorkshire became popular as a new sensibility towards the poetics of landscape spread among the middle and upper classes. Picnics and even weddings were held in the graveyards of ruined churches, as nineteenth-century Britons reflected on the beauties and virtues of late medieval society.[4]

In similar if more limited fashion, industrial ruins have become denkmals, occasions for reflection. In the nineteenth century, tourists visited industrial sites such as the coal fields of Mauch Chunk in eastern Pennsylvania to enjoy new technologies at work in a magnificent industrial setting, and to reaffirm their faith in the course of progress. By way of contrast, to at least one firm of late-twentieth-century architects, the "coal mines, canal and even the railroad, now in decay, seem to form part of the Romantic landscape. . . . Symbols of human battle against an overwhelming nature now seem to return themselves to nature as Romantic ruins."[5]

Thus, while early-twentieth-century architects spoke of the machine age and the machine aesthetic, late-twentieth-century architects, artists, and photographers find aesthetic and philosophical content in ruined machine complexes such as abandoned mills and collieries. Such structures have a stark, imposing effect on the landscape not unlike that of ancient religious monuments. The visual parallel has not been lost on those who are able to exploit it in moody photographs and illustrations.

Beyond the aesthetic effect, the identification of industrial ruins as sites of reflection, not just for artists, but also for tourists, led to opportunities for philosophizing about the power of humanity against nature and the process of industrial decline. Thus the popular text entitled *Discovering Britain: Where to See the Best of Our Countryside* directs tourists to a derelict Welsh colliery, to be appreciated as "a monument to the old way of life. . . . Work was hard and dangerous, but the community was close-knit and there was the sense of the hills not far away."[6] In the States, industrial ruins at Harper's Ferry, West Virginia, are similarly evocative of changing fortunes within a splendid natural setting.

The Integrated Object

Many of the artifacts and structures of industrial society remain integrated within the fabric of postindustrial society. Some of these retain their original function such as Victorian water towers that still store water, sewage systems that continue their work of disposal. Some such structures are, however, singled out as objects for reflection and veneration, as industrial archaeologists and preservationists make claims for their historic and/or aesthetic significance.

Sometimes this process entails minimal intervention, affixing a bronze plaque to the facade, carrying out basic maintenance. In other instances major campaigns must be waged involving issues of selection and legitimation and the garnering of public and financial support. For many, industrial society is a world we have lost—and thankfully so. Historian Tamara Hareven notes that among those most opposed to the preservation of the New England textile mills are the former workers and their families, who would rather forget than remember how the mills ran the town and their day-to-day lives.[7]

Because of financial issues, many industrial structures are reintegrated by being recycled through the process of adaptive reuse. Mills, factories, and warehouses are converted into condominiums, offices, and shopping malls. Corbusier's modernist ethic, which wanted to make the home a "machine for living in," has been replaced by a new ethic that values history as well as technology. Former industrial factories are given face lifts through adaptive reuses; architects and clients appreciate the cozy warmth of their exposed brick walls and the sense of continuity they provide. The heavy manufacturing equipment that once filled these structures is long gone, replaced by light industrial equipment, including food processors, copying machines, and laser beam cash registers.

The Exhibited Object

Once an industrial object is singled out for attention, it can either frame or be framed.[8] It can form the interpretive core or the surround. London's Science Museum is itself a late-industrial object, part of Prince Albert's efforts to spread knowledge of the benefits of science and the achievements of technology. The museum provides an appropriate frame for exhibited objects that complete the narrative. In the museum's entrance stand three select objects: a 1903 Humberette automobile, a 1912 handloom with jacquard pattern weaving, and a complicated, special-purpose drilling, boring, and tapping machine (1983). The presumed ability of such objects to speak for themselves is reinforced by a backdrop of quotations, such as William Gilbert's (1540–1603) advice to "look for knowledge not in books, but in things themselves."

Science museums take objects from their original sites and recontextualize them within a highly artificial structure.[9] They strategically incorporate objects into narratives meant to reveal to the viewer the complexity and diversity of science and technology.

Science museums can be read as general advertisements for industrial society, holding up its varied goods for examination and adulation. They can also add new functions to the old, as has the Kew Bridge Steam Museum, among many other museums engaged

in imaginative fundraising. Located in a nineteenth-century pump-
ing station, the Steam Museum advertises itself as the ideal location
for filming and also as a site for product launches, corporate entertainments, private concerts, and other social functions.

Other museums function as specific advertisements for specific
products. In the West, the development of industrial society went
hand-in-hand with the rise of capitalist enterprise. Many contemporary corporations have early entrepreneurial antecedents, with
the accompanying artifacts that no one quite got around to destroying. These artifacts and structures now have considerable tourist
potential. Bass Brewery has opened a museum of brewing, Royal
Brierly (founded 1776) has a museum of crystal, and Wedgwood has
a museum and visitor center tracing the history of the works. Mer-
chandise outlets are usually close by.

Living Museums as Complex Objects

More comprehensive efforts at recontextualization include the
massive restoration of original sites, including whole communities,
and the imaginative creation of new ones. Industrial sites, while still
not as popular as nostalgic, agrarian villages, also run the gamut of
authenticity. One interesting case is Henry Ford's restoration of
the Edison Laboratories, which involved removing them from their
original site at Menlo Park, New Jersey, and transporting them to
the imaginary community Ford created at Greenfield, Michigan.
Besides paying homage to his personal hero, Ford sought by this
means to instill in America's youth a proper appreciation of and
respect for the course of industrial progress.[10]

A second major example involved the National Park Service's
restoration of a major ironfounding community at Hopewell, Pennsylvania. Begun in the late 1930, this restoration is a major site and
includes charcoal hearths and cooling shed, furnaces, cast houses,
cleaning shed and blacksmith shop, community store, ironmaster's
mansion, and tenant houses, among other structures. In the summer, costumed interpreters reenact social roles associated with
ironfounding and with everyday life in the 1830s and 1840s, when
the furnace was in its most productive period.

In contrast to the early engagement of the American government at Hopewell, the British government appeared reluctant to re-create the industrial past. As a result, "industrial archaeology" became a more explicit crusade against official representations of the national past and of the image of the preindustrial, pastoral ideal. This crusade was directed both against manufacturers, who, sensitive to charges of being retrogressive, destroyed many earlier structures, and also against government officials, who were slow to pass enabling legislation and to contribute necessary financial support to preservation efforts.

The critical breakthrough occurred when Allied Ironfounders began preserving the structures it had inherited as the distant heir to Abraham Darby's original eighteenth-century ironworks in the Severn Valley, west of Birmingham. The site could not be more significant, containing as it did the foundry where the breakthrough from charcoal to coke-fired furnaces had occurred. This freed iron production from dependence on extensive forests and opened the path to more sophisticated forms of iron production. This was also the site of Darby's famous 1779 iron bridge, an enduring monument to the skill of early ironworkers. For such reasons, Ironbridge Gorge was and is rightly seen as the birthplace of the Industrial Revolution. But it was a birthplace largely neglected until 1960, when the company and interested historians and archaeologists began to reconstruct its monuments and interpret them to the public.

Today, Ironbridge Gorge is a major tourist attraction. Extending for four miles along the Severn river, it comprises a number of major and minor sites. Among the major sites are the Museum of Iron and Darby Furnace, Rosehill House, the Museum of the River (formerly the Severn warehouse), the Coalport China Museum, the Jackfield Tile Museum, and the iron bridge itself, in the center of the gorge. The most popular attraction is Blists Hill Open Air Museum. an imaginative recreation of a late-nineteenth-century industrial community, complete with costumed interpreters. The site is not authentic: the structures are a mix of the authentic imported and newly constructed, and the content, with jovial interpreters mingling with tourists, lacks a certain authenticity, the significance of which will be discussed shortly.

Following the success of Ironbridge, a number of other living museums have been created. The nearby Black Country Museum makes the Industrial Revolution sound positively inviting. Its brochure encourages you to "take a trip on an electric tramcar past a working replica of the world's first steam engine and a typical Black Country pit to the village by the canal. Wander into the many houses, shops and other buildings where costumed demonstrators offer a warm welcome as they . . . transport you back to another era." By contrast, a more serious and sedate approach is followed at Styal, in the English Midlands, where the National Trust and the Quarry Bank Mill Trust have preserved both the village and the cotton mill complex that was the center of life.

In America, perhaps the leading industrial representation is Lowell, Massachusetts, where extensive interpretive sites are located throughout the city and are connected for tourists by maps and a choice of tours. The opening of exhibits at Boott Mill in June 1992 provided a new centerpiece. Unlike other factory exhibits, which feature one prototype of each machine, Boott Mill's first floor is a whole weaveroom filled with ninety automatic looms, of which several produce cloth, while the rest contribute to the clatter and din through simulated operation. Other exhibits describe the rise of the factory system, the history of Lowell mills, the development of the mill technology, and the decline of the industry in Lowell. Another major attraction are the tours of Lowell's distinctive canal system. The canal rides, while educational, share the pleasurable quality of our next category.

The Nostalgic Leisure Experience

Among the most popular recontextualizations of industrial machinery is their conversion into nostalgic leisure experiences. This is particularly true of forms of transportation. In Britain, both the National Trust and various private interests have been involved in restoring old canal networks as the popularity of canal cruising by barge and boat continues to grow. In America, trains, canals, and even steamboats have enjoyed a similar resurgence and tourist popularity.

Before manufacturers ever saw the potential in old factories, railway enthusiasts set about acquiring the means to restore old steam engines, cars, and tracks. America has its examples of these old steam lines, especially in New England and the far West, such as the line originating in Durango, Colorado. But they are a major passion in Britain, land of train spotters. One of the largest of these operations, the Severn Valley Railway, runs the sixteen-mile distance from Bridgnorth to Kidderminster and provides many idyllic views of open countryside, restored village stations, and the steam engines themselves.

An unusual collection of steam vehicles is found at Bressingham, Norfolk. Sharing billing with one of Britain's leading horticultural centers, the Bloom nursery, the collection of working steam-powered locomotives, carrousels, and farm equipment offers a vivid instance of the "machine in the garden."[11] The attractions of agrarian and industrial orders are combined, however uneasily and artificially, as they can be in a tourist experience. Down in coastal Folkestone, a water-powered lift takes bathers up and down from cliff to beach, while to the north in the Lake District, a restored steam gondola silently plies the waters of Lake Windermere.

Motor museums are also popular. Birmingham's Autoworld is set in a converted Victorian paper mill and the Midland Motor Museum is located in a country estate. Across the Atlantic a small, independently run motor museum in Sturbridge, Massachusetts, benefits from the immense popularity of Old Sturbridge Village.

▨ Social Motives

As industrial preservation grows in presence and popularity, it is worth asking what explicit and implicit social motives lie behind it.[12] A reading of industrial preservation's apologists on both sides of the Atlantic suggests the following list of motives.

Importance to History

The preservation of industrial structures is most often justified in terms of their historical importance. Among those concerned, there's a sense of impending loss if care is not taken to safeguard the object.[13] Future generations, the argument goes, will be impoverished if they do not have the direct link to the object; if they cannot see for themselves. The sense of urgency is spurred by actual losses, especially when campaigns for their preservation had been mounted. In Britain, a critical moment came with the loss of the Euston Arch outside of the Euston train station. In the States, the destruction of New York's magnificent Pennsylvania Station awakened many to the impending loss of other historic structures. Following the Euston Arch demolition in 1961, the Council of British Archaeology realized "the urgent need to get important monuments recognized, listed, documented and where possible, preserved."[14]

In the States there had already been some government involvement in industrial preservation. The opportunistic aspect of much preservation is evident in Hopewell's claim to historic significance, for it is admitted that Hopewell "is neither the oldest, the biggest, nor the last charcoal iron furnace in blast in the United States, but it is a site about which much is known and whose extensive remains are of interest to students and casual visitors alike."[15]

Given the complicated development of and interdependent relations between industrial societies, curators and guides at historic sites take pains to point out exactly what the site's *specific* claim to importance is. Pawtucket, Rhode Island's Slater Mill can be considered the birthplace of the factory system in America; Saugus, Massachusetts, the beginning of America's iron industry. Lowell is notable for bringing several currents together, including the idea of the industrial town, a significant experiment in women's rights, and the extensive implementation of turbine and other breakthrough technology.

Importance to history is often conflated with the importance to the nation. Like patriotic shrines, industrial sites provide opportunities for people to pay respect to the economic achievements of the nation.[16] This impulse may get stronger as industrial might grows weaker. Anthony Burton suggests that the British find it appealing to look back to a time when Britain led the world, when, as Burton writes, "today we palpably do not hold any such position in the affairs of nations."[17] The "nostalgic attachment" of which Burton writes is evident in the Museum of Advertising and Packaging, whose two hundred thousand objects are described as forming a colorful "tribute to the vigor and inventiveness of British manufacturing industry."

Pedagogic Motive

Industrial objects are meant to be educational. Schools and youth organizations represent a major market for both industrial sites and industrial exhibits in science museums. Extensive teaching materials have been prepared to help teachers reinforce in the classroom the lessons learned on the site.

The pedagogic motive was a key one for industrial leaders such as Henry Ford, who believed children should learn their history not from books but from historical objects. Parents who include such visits in their holiday plans take pride in furthering their children's education. The point is driven home by tourist promotions, both in written and video form, that seem inevitably to feature awestruck and incredibly well-behaved children, breathing in history.

Beyond such explicit lessons in history, science, and technology lies the "hidden curriculum." Industrial narratives have moral content. In these interpretations, emphasis is traditionally placed on the personal and moral qualities of inventors and early industrialists—their ingenuity, creativity, and enterprise—and their sheer hard work. Sometimes, as in the introductory film to the Ironbridge exhibits, explicit mention is made of the need to recapture and reinstill such qualities today if Western nations such as Britain and the United States are to emerge from the postindustrial doldrums. Visitors to exhibits on the nineteenth century learn how hard life was then and are told how they should all be thankful for the many achievements of modern science and technology. Not the least of these, according to London's Science Museum, is the replacement of a world view based on "terror and superstition" with a scientific world view based on "wonder and understanding." This narrative is one way through which science becomes its own ideology, a process that is evident in industrial exhibits.[18]

The Romance of the Machine

"I sell . . . what all the world desires to have—POWER." This quotation, from Matthew Boulton, James Watts's partner, greets visitors as they enter the Great Hall of London's Science Museum. Power is indeed behind much of the appeal of industrial preservation. Industrialization gave us machine power, which was vastly greater than manpower or horsepower. In the process we became, as Freud has argued, "prosthetic gods," using machines as extensions of our own body, achieving things that would never before have been possible.[19]

Science museums recognize this process explicitly. Their "Power Halls" have been the traditional, primary means of interpreting the Industrial Revolution. The National Museum of American History tried to break away from this imaging, or at least complement exhibits of major machinery by emphasizing how industrial technology worked as a force for social change. The point is explicitly made in an exhibit's title: "Engines of Change."

The appeal of industrial machines is not simply that they speak of power, but rather that they speak of a power that is understandable. Marx believed that capitalism alienated workers from their tools. But, compared to today's microchips and lasers, the technology behind the early industrial machines is much more open to examination and human comprehension. Compared to the present level of technology where everyday appliances from digital watches to car engines remain black boxes to most consumers, early steam engines seem remarkably user friendly. The machines themselves are given human, especially stereotypically male, qualities. They are robust. They display a rugged self confidence. Sometimes, they were even given names.

Social Maturity

The desire to return to the agrarian past has often been related to a desire to return to one's childhood.[20] The preindustrial period appears as a nation's innocent childhood, a veritable Eden, in which people of all social statuses happily coexisted. In Britain, this image is reinforced by the appealing image of well-kept villages nestling in the countryside. In America, it is the Jeffersonian image of a nation of independent farmers: the garden before the machine.

But the machine did arrive, and with it the need to leave the garden, to "grow up" personally and socially. For preservation activists, if not their audiences, industrial preservation represents a recognition of industrial society as an important, if painful, stage in a nation's history. Their desire is to free it from infantile psychic projections and nostalgic representations.

In his review of industrial archaeology in Britain, Anthony Burton singles out for admiration the treatment of technical and social change in the cotton mill and village at Styal. "Here," writes Burton, "we can appreciate the buildings and restored machinery, while at the same time we are never allowed to forget the often grim condition under which the men, women and children who tended these machines worked." Burton goes on to emphasize that such presentations are needed not simply to correct the nostalgic view of the past, but also to convey the relevance of the past to the present and future.[21] In his review of the Smithsonian's "Engines of Change" exhibit, Michael Stratton criticizes the oversanitized quality of the displays, singling out in particular a model workshop powered by a steam engine. "The workshop is brilliantly lighted and spotless . . . and the white plastic machinist looks like a ghost serving in a fast food outlet." Stratton suggests that, "Given that visitors are kept out of the workshop by barriers, why can there not be a good layer of industrial grime and evidence of human life introduced into the display?"[22]

▨ *The New Social History*

As the Stratton critique suggests, the professional standards for industrial preservation are under debate. The earlier, heroic school of interpretation, with its emphasis on the brilliance of inventors, the daring of entrepreneurs, and the romance of the technology itself, is being challenged by professionals exposed to the new social history taught in colleges and universities.

Meaning has become the explicit object of contest. To appreciate and evaluate an exhibit, you have to deduce whose side it's on. Bob West sharply attacks the Blists Hill village reconstruction at Ironbridge for its inauthentic representation of the industrial working class. West focuses on the sawmill, contrasting the representation with his own personal experience. "An actual sawmill is pervaded by an atmosphere of 'masculinity': risk, competition, aggressiveness, and sexual innuendo are lightened by humor and male friendships. There is real danger in a sawmill, the noise is deafening, and the sense of isolation acute. Accidents are common but men struggle not to show fear, castigating it in others; they minimize their injuries, and put a brave face on crushed hands and lost fingers."[23]

While the exhibit demonstrators were able to explain the technology of the sawmill, they were not prepared to consider the social relations of production. West writes, "What angered me about the sawmill and the woodworking shop was that the 'reality' it produced actively disorganized, and thus rendered illegitimate, any alternative account of what this experience of work amounts to."[24]

To some, this constitutes a form of "symbolic violence" to working class imaginations and interpretations.[25] To avoid it and the broader charges of inaccuracy and inauthenticity, preservation professionals increasingly create narratives featuring workers as well as owners, and represent the costs as well as the benefits of industrialization. Guides are instructed to explain the health dangers associated with heavy machinery as well as the social and economic dislocations that resulted from industrialization.

This trend is now so much in evidence that some professionals wonder if they haven't erred too far in the opposite direction and written the owners and entrepreneurs out of their industrial narratives.[26] The most professional guides take pains to emphasize that industrial work was not all hazard and that wage labor was not the first form of exploitation. Traditional forms of farm and craft work contained their own dangers and economic inequalities.

Even if the curators wanted to represent sawmill labor as West remembers it, there are limits to how far they could go down this path. The raw masculinity he describes is not the usual subject for tours of schoolchildren and senior citizens or for family outings. Layers of dirt and grime violate tourist expectations, and serious questioning of industrialism's costs runs counter to the ideology of many political and economic interests involved in preservation. It is to this and related issues that we now turn.

Social Issues

Social Progressivism

Curators aim for ever new levels of professionalism, treating their work as science and respecting the objects of science and technology under their care. This does not preclude their using these objects to tell narratives. If there has been one overarching narrative in these exhibits until recent years, it has been the saga of social progressivism. Showing what it was that made America great was the explicit goal of such major industrialists and amateur preservationists as Henry Ford and Albert O. Wells. Others followed suit, in small local museums and major institutions.

Some museums recognize that industrial progress brought discontents, but emphasize the overall progressive course. In the "Society" section of the London Science Museum's brochure, the problem is handled thus: "Above all it is the higher living standards which only an industrialized society seems able to support that have made the most difference. Though industrialization brings far-from-trivial ills of its own, among its undoubted benefits is the fact that, in Britain at least, twenty times fewer children now die before the age of five than was the case a century ago."

It is hard to argue against saving children. But nowhere is it suggested, for example, that this improvement in the standard of living may be destroying the ecological basis necessary for human life itself.

Even when curators try to balance the presentation, the objects themselves may speak more loudly than the words printed on wall plaques and in guidebooks. As one critic, Bernard S. Finn writes, "Objects *look* progressive, and audiences tend to translate technical progress to mean social progress."[27] For example, while an exhibit on household technology used labels and advertisement reproductions to argue that women had been manipulated by manufacturers, the objects themselves, viewed together, suggested that quaintness had yielded to efficiency.[28] As suggested in my introduction, this perception has the effect of ironing out all the contradictions of history: the social progressivist narrative has an inevitability about it, and the tourist leaves the exhibit with a Panglossian sense of living in the best of all possible worlds.

Who Pays?

Usually, the progressivist narrative does not arise solely out of the objects. Rather, it may receive strong encouragement from political and economic interests. To the extent that museums are arenas in which a nation presents its achievements to its citizens and foreign visitors, governments have an interest in how those achievements are interpreted. But government support is often uncertain. The withdrawal of much government support during World War II was, as we have seen, one key reason behind the founding of the American National Trust. Thatcher's government provided another instance of half-begun projects suffering the withdrawal of funds. At the Kelham Island Industrial Museum, in Sheffield, funding cuts meant the postponement of a planned expansion of this museum devoted to the steel industry and its allied crafts. In addition, there was no money to begin a training program for apprentices to replace the remaining elder master craftsmen, who demonstrated their skills to museum visitors.

Typically, when government support for preservation projects decreases, curators are strongly encouraged to seek out corporate sponsorship. Kelham Island may become a trust, the better to garner such sponsorship. At least one historian attached to Sheffield University worries that such sponsorship may encourage a sanitizing and a prettifying of this essential local industry, and advises the would-be tourist to visit soon, "before the emollient hand of the heritage industry transforms it into something altogether more soothing."[29]

The impact of such sponsorship may be minimal—the inclusion of the company name on entry plaques and tourist brochures. Or it may be major: The founder of the Museum of Advertising and Packaging has eagerly courted corporate sponsors and expressed a willingness to devote whole halls or exhibits to the development of one company's packaging and advertising over time, for example, a Cadbury's Hall of Chocolate. Where a museum is attached to one manufacturer, such as at Corning Glass or Wedgwood, its advertising function is clear, and a balanced presentation of industrialism's costs and benefits can hardly be expected.

The money for exhibits comes from government agencies, foundations, and corporate sponsors. It also comes from the paying public. Staff salaries may be tied to entrance fees and souvenir sales, one means of guaranteeing that the staff is interested in public reaction and caters to it.

The visiting public wants exhibits to be credible. But it also wants its own ideology reaffirmed. Dean MacCannell has identified this ideology in America as forming a hymn to the differentiation of society, "E Pluribus Unum" displayed and reconstructed.[30] In Britain, also, class conflict used to be seldom emphasized. At Ironbridge, the ironmaster's mansion is a major stop, while worker housing receives scant mention in a dark corner of the Museum of Iron.

But this is changing. At Styal, for example, the mill exhibits stress both the technology and related social history. Interpreters at the Apprentices House describe the harsh conditions under which boys and girls served, but also that Styal's conditions were no worse, and in some ways better, than those found elsewhere. The patriarchal class relationship between owners and workers is emphasized throughout, as is the workers' poverty. Styal has enlarged reproductions of correspondence between workers and owners, in which the workers beg for small favors. The budgets of families where both parents and children worked in the mill are also featured.

Worker history deserves as much scholarly attention and curatorial acumen as any other subject. Even as new exhibits are mounted, however, concerns are beginning to be expressed that worker interests are not being fully served. Curators and historians set their own high professional standards, and provide each other's best and most critical audience. An exhibit on "The Working People of Richmond: Life and Labor in an Industrial City, 1865-1920," held at the Valentine Museum, Richmond, Virginia, drew just such critical attention. In a review, Peter Liebhold, a specialist from the Smithsonian, applauded the popular appeal of living history presentations in which actors and actresses impersonated an Irish-American bartender, a tobacco stemmer, and an iron roller. But Liebhold was critical about the more traditional exhibit of related objects, which he considered "text heavy and academic in tone." While recognizing the museum director's desire to maintain strong academic standards, Liebhold worried that curators might be simply trading the old social elitism for a new, academic elitism. Reflecting on the difficulties of maintaining scholarly standards while avoiding a dry, academic tone, and also of the dangers of turning worker history exhibits into "a poor-quality copy of Disney World," Liebhold counseled curators on the advisability of learning "to democratize their voice as well as their message."[31]

What will be the impact of the new social history on industrial site audiences? Will it attract more of a working-class audience, or will its earnestness scare them away in search of amusements? The tension between education and entertainment is a major one facing curators of industrial sites.

Education versus Entertainment

Most industrial exhibits seem inherently less fanciful than other historic representations. Only the nostalgic leisure experiences, the steam boats and trains, the canal boats and beach lifts, are devoted to play. The idea that industrial exhibits are, or should be, serious business is reinforced by the professional discourse in which claims to authenticity are central.

But an exhibit can be authentic and credible without being pleasing, educational without being entertaining. To avoid the risk of boring and losing its public, the Chicago Museum of Science and Industry pioneered the interactive exhibits now widely accepted in similar institutions. Visitors no longer simply read labels and study objects. Instead, they pick up telephones to hear recorded explanations and push buttons to set machinery in motion. Actors in eighteenth-century costume waylay families to explain the latest advances in steam engines. The most popular section of London's

Science Museum, the Launch Pad, is a sizable playroom with brightly colored play structures, each of which embodies some scientific principle.

Videos are also used at many industrial sites to prepare tourists for the exhibits and also to send them back into the world with a coherent and pleasing impression. These films act as frames for the exhibits, and are also commercials for the exhibits, and play a key role in tourist management. They reaffirm the importance of the industrial exhibit or site. Through evocative imagery they help tourists imagine the earlier industrial context, which can not be fully re-created in reality. They tell visitors both what they will see and how they should see it.

Judging by visitor response, the most entertaining exhibit at Ironbridge is the Blists Hill representation of an 1890s industrial community. There, tourists can watch a mine-shaft operator use steam-powered machinery to raise and lower the cage. They can tour the chemist's shop, the bakery, and even the candlestick maker's, and listen to the story told by the squatter in his cottage on the edge of the village. They can drink in the nineteenth-century pub and pay for their pint with old currency picked up at the nineteenth-century Lloyd's Bank near the village entrance. A genial policeman is happy to handcuff children for amusing family photographs. The major ironworks (authentic to the site) sit dull and brooding by comparison to all the activity on the largely inauthentic High Street.

Curators recognize the limits of what such exhibits can achieve in authenticity. One Ironbridge curator commented that if you ask the old-timers what it used to be like in the Gorge, they will begin by saying, "Well, it was black. . . ."

In Blists Hill, it is not black. Both air and streets are clean, no drunks congregate outside the pubs, and no whores solicit among the crowd. Small industrial exhibits can be put into operation, but all the negative by-products of industrialization, from air pollution to class conflict, are missing in such staged communities. Even Bob West, who argues for more authenticity at Blists Hill and other industrial representations, recognizes that one cannot in good conscience expose tourists or interpreters to the actual health risks of nineteenth-century industrial production in the name of authenticity.

Recognizing the misrepresentation in such historic representations, some preservation professionals attempt to correct the visual impression through the written word. At Ironbridge's Museum of the River, visitors learn that industrialization had its costs in pollution and disease. Most of the critique is related safely to the past, with present problems being treated with the "can do" spirit ("if we all join in"). Still, visitors experience this exhibit as a "downer" and rank it among their least favorite of the major exhibits.

Curators also use guidebooks to describe those unpleasant smells and noises that can not be included in the gentle and safe tourist landscape. The historian describing Hopewell Furnace writes, "When the furnace was in blast, normally 24 hours a day for most of the year, the village throbbed with life: the roaring of the furnace stack, the shouts of the workmen, the water wheel monotonously clanking round and round, wagons creaking along with ore, the cast house bell periodically calling the moulders back to work. Dust, soot, and furnace odor fouled the air."[32]

But there is nothing like the real thing. When Saugus Ironworks puts its water wheels into motion, tourists are stunned by the racket produced. When the hammer operates, they are warned ahead of time to cover their ears. Without the noise and smell of industrial production, restored sites seem too often like movie sets. Even Robert Owen's restored utopian industrial community at Lanark, Scotland, seems more pretty than pathbreaking to some visitors. Despite the efforts of guides to stress what was innovatory, the effect is like television newscast in which the visual of a staged political "photo opportunity" overpowers any critical commentary provided by newscasters.

Knowledge versus Ignorance

Related to the issue of entertainment versus education is the question of how much knowledge curators can expect of their public. Compared to nostalgic displays of village crafts, the story of the industrial revolution is a particularly complex one to tell. It spans not just villages, but regions and even nations. People, material, and markets are interwoven in ever-changing relationships. Even select aspects of this transformation require serious attention.

At Ironbridge, curators have planned an exhibit on economic geology, which will emphasize both the importance of raw materials and the effect of their extraction on the landscape. The exhibit would cover the geological process of subsidence and the difficulties involved in reclamation. But they worry whether tourists will share their enthusiasm or experience it as just another downer.

The old-fashioned museum strategy was to make certain demands upon the visitor, who was expected to come with some knowledge and prepared to make sense of the exhibits. Some specialty museums still stress the primacy of the object, which is presented without much accompanying fanfare. At the American Precision Museum in Windsor, Vermont, the machine-tool collection is presented in a plain historic structure.

Other technical museums, however, reflect their origins in trade fairs, with which they share an emphasis on the "superficial and the spectacular," as well as the same uncritical approach to progress.[33] Science museums, once stuffy repositories, have received public-pleasing facelifts and even been criticized for using "retail aesthetics" to attract tourists who otherwise would not bother visiting. To defenders, this is a small price to pay for the benefits of attracting a broader audience.

Thus, specific aspects of the industrial past can be expropriated and given different interpretations. These interpretations depend in part on the material *and* ideal interests of the social actors involved. One of the most important shifts in interpretation is being created by historians trained in the new social history. But their worker-based narratives encounter the same problems of selection and emphasis as the earlier owner-entrepreneur narratives.

The scale and breadth of exhibits are of crucial importance. In relatively small-scale exhibits, several of the conflicts outlined above can be satisfactorily resolved. For example, the Mattatuck Museum in Waterbury, Connecticut, features a walk-through exhibit on the brass manufacturing industry, which once dominated the local economy. Because of its singular emphasis, the exhibit manages to present both the technology of brass manufacture and the social relations that developed around it. The exhibit also contrasts the living standard of an owner and a worker by depicting house interior rooms that might be associated with each social class. Enlarged maps and photographs outline the city's changing borders, architecture, and ethnic composition.

When the scope of representation broadens, so too do the problems in interpretation. At a complex exhibit like Lowell, visitors viewing the fast-paced introductory film may come away with a very sketchy sense of Lowell's industrial history and an even less clear sense of its relationship to the industrial Northeast's current economic problems. How much of the sketch is then filled in will depend on which tours the visitors follow and on how much time they are willing to spend learning about the town's complex industrial and ethnic history. When exhibits deal with nation-wide phenomena, problems again increase. An exhibit such as the "Engines of Change" in Washington must be highly selective, packing a range of examples and case studies in industrialization into a very small space.

The debate over industrial history is important because it is also a debate over how we will explain social inequality. Social class can be interpreted as part of nature, as a process of natural selection through which owners, inventors, and entrepreneurs rose to the top while workers stayed at the bottom. Or, social class can be seen as a system of exploitation, in which the ruling class actively prevented the working class from rising. Social inequality today can be seen as a legacy of the industrial past, which we are in the process of overcoming. This tends to be a latent interpretation in America, where over 90 percent of the population self-identify with the middle class, and where the financial press tries to sell one and all on the idea of "building wealth." Or, social class can be seen as deeply woven into the fabric of society. Such tends to be the case in Great Britain, where social class is a recognized part of nearly every social and political debate.

Within this context of contemporary issues and debates, industrial representations offer possibilities for recognition, re-creation, and experimentation. On an individual level, many visitors to industrial sites are making personal pilgrimages into family history. Some have grandparents or great grandparents who worked in factories or collieries. These descendants come to reclaim the past and to pay respect. Industrial cities, such as Leeds, that once looked down on their past are now attempting to tell their stories.

Industrial representations provide an appropriate setting for contemplating social and economic change. Two major industrial sites—Lowell, Massachusetts, and Lanark, Scotland—were once social experiments. To some extent, capitalism itself was an experiment—one that has, like the socialist experiment, come up with mixed results. In the waning years of the twentieth century, both nations must respond to a range of social and economic problems. Perhaps the sites of our industrial origin hold within them clues to innovative solutions.

War and ▨ CHAPTER 5
Remembrance

*Jackson didn't sleep here . . . but you can.
Fredericksburg's charming Civil War Era Inn
was neither open nor built when Stonewall
Jackson, Robert E. Lee, Ulysses S. Grant and
McClellan fought the Civil War and the famous
"Battle of Fredericksburg." But that hasn't
stopped us from re-enacting "Living History"
and furnishing our 30 rooms and suites with
high, solid wood queen size beds of the Victorian period, marble-topped dressers, and
original prints and paintings of Civil War
days.* —Advertisement in Fredericksburg,
Virginia, tourist brochure

The inn with the "Stonewall Jackson" honeymoon suite may be
new, but the preservation of Civil War battlefields such as
Fredericksburg is long standing. Unlike industrial preservation,
preserving armaments and battlefields has long been considered a
task of national importance. Like industrial preservation, however, it now involves a difficult set of political and social issues. It
was an age less ambiguous than our own that gave responsibility for
the preservation of American Civil War battlefields to the Department of War, now, of course, renamed the Department of Defense.

Just as industrial preservation invites different social class
interpretations, war preservation invites interpretations other than

the purely patriotic and glorious. The interpretations of the victorious differ from those of the vanquished, civilian perspectives may differ from those of the armed forces, and women may also view war differently than men to the extent that it affects them differently.

Thus, if war is politics continued by other means, preservation is also politics continued by other means. These "means" revolve around the act of commemoration. Curators have become increasingly sensitive about the political content of their exhibits as social groups have begun to contest interpretations. Today, serious challenges have arisen to the "Hell Bent for Glory" aspect of many earlier presentations. We now question the aesthetics attached to crisp, colored uniforms, the swords displayed in pretty patterns, and the awe inspired by technological might and land "consecrated with blood." In the process, however, we are creating an alternate aesthetic. Like it or not, the exhibited war object acquires aesthetic value, even if this value resembles the grotesque.

In addition to the political problems in interpreting acts of war, there is also a whole range of problems relating to the nature of the objects and their interpretation. Putting aside fancy uniforms and gleaming swords, modern war relics are not necessarily pretty. More often they are ugly, rusted, grimy reminders of death and destruction. The barbed wire of twentieth-century battlefields is a far cry from the privet hedging of Colonial representations or the attractive facades of Britain's "best kept" villages.

Yet battlefields and war museums are a popular destination for family holidays, school trips, and individual pilgrimages. The act of commemoration is an important one for society, especially where what is being commemorated is supreme sacrifice made for the nation.

Sacrifice is an important concept and considered crucial to a nation's survival. If people are no longer willing to sacrifice for their nation, can the nation long exist? Commemoration serves to encourage future acts of sacrifice, as it promises the would-be heroes that they will not die in vain and that they will be remembered by future generations. It is an unwritten pact between the dead, the living, and the unborn, and it is enacted through social rituals— the acts of commemoration.

Battlefields are also arenas where social values are contested. To have social significance, battles must be interpreted, in part, as moral dramas, not just struggles for advantage, for more chips. Even struggles with a clear political or economic object are justified by concepts such as "God's will," "justice," and/or "national honor." Which lessons are drawn from these dramas depends not just on what happened on the battlefield, in the past, but on political dramas being enacted in the present, and on which social forces are currently in contention. Some Americans, for example, believe the lesson in Pearl Harbor was that America must never again be caught off guard militarily. Other Americans see this national tragedy as teaching broader social lessons, most notably the dangers in confounding race and nationality, as evident in America's incarceration of Japanese citizens. To still others, Pearl Harbor is a symbol reminding Americans to be wary of the Japanese: their present economic strength is as much a threat as was their former military might.

The basic facts of the past military encounter remain and continue to signify; what changes is the interpretative frame that is constructed around these events. In considering the interpretation of this and other moments in military history, we need to ask how much is included within the interpretive frame (the specific event or the broader social surround), who is doing the interpreting, and for what purpose, however explicit or implicit. In the twentieth century, everyone has, in some way, been touched by war. The different relationships of people to war events are critical to the processes of interpretation and commemoration.[1]

Before considering the range of historic representations of war, we must first review certain basic differences and similarities between Great Britain and the United States in terms of their military history. Neither nation was part of the land wars of World War I and World War II. Britain was, however, directly threatened and attacked by air, with the massive shelling of London and other sites such as Coventry.

Both nations fought other wars abroad, declared and undeclared. Both nations experienced a civil war: the United States in the mid-nineteenth century, Great Britain in the mid-seventeenth century. The United States also had its War of Rebellion, or of Independence, depending on how you look at it. Britain has a far longer history of wars—with their fortifications dating back to the Romans. Historical evidence of these fortifications is still preserved.

Thus the experience of Great Britain and the United States is significantly different from that of France or Germany, where the land battles of World War I and II were fought, or from many Third World nations, which have fought to overthrow colonialism. Points of contrast with these other societies will be drawn throughout this discussion.

Recontextualizations: Isolation versus Integration

After World War II, a few of the big guns, silent, remained on British beaches. Now they have all been cleared away. Who wants to live next to one of those, unsafe as they are for children and unattractive to all? What remains are the machine gun bunkers, now frequently shelter for lovers. The bunkers have joined the Martello towers, dating from the Napoleonic era, as evidence of Britain's historic fears of invasion from the Continent.

Several of the Continental battlefields have been preserved, notably those on the beaches at Normandy and amid the forests of Verdun. But leaving armaments lying about as isolated monuments is not a popular preservation strategy. More often they are moved to public places: the big gun on the promontory, the Civil War cannon in the town square, the tank outside the armory.

In contrast to the isolated industrial ruin in the rural landscape, we have the interesting and evocative integrated civic ruin. Cities more than countrysides were the targets of bombers. Some cities have left bombed-out buildings as reminders of war or testimonials for peace. One of the most famous is the Coventry cathedral, where a modern cathedral has been built into the carefully preserved skeleton of the former religious masterwork. London also contained a civic ruin, the remnant of a church near St. Paul's, which itself miraculously survived the Blitz. To some, the moral lesson is that God really is English. It is worth noting that, within this relatively small class of civic ruins, the majority are religious structures. Such structures are most readily associated with moral values and with the idea of a moral community. As such, they speak for a morality that transcends political exigency and that does not underestimate the human costs of war.

Many British cities and towns are built in and around military ruins. Indeed, one of the earliest purposes for establishment of towns was as bastions defending territory. In cities such as Colchester, stretches of Roman wall remind residents of the town's earlier military role. This historic role continues today, with the stationing of army regiments in this East Anglian garrison town. English Heritage holds responsibility for many historic forts, where interpretation places a high premium on historical accuracy. At other sites not under the care of English Heritage, less emphasis is placed on accuracy and more on popularity. Fort Luton, located southeast of London, advertises a side attraction of cuddly bunnies!

In the United States, a number of midwestern cities owe their origin to their role as forts, although it is largely the forts outside urban areas that have been preserved and interpreted for tourists. In other towns, the original fort was never preserved but a new one built, sometimes considerably more picturesque in order to fit tourist notions of a "real fort."[2]

American Civil War battlefields have always attracted tourists, ever more so since the airing of a popular public television series on the Civil War. Towns and surrounding areas benefit from the tourist wave, even as the integrity of the landscape is threatened by tourist services and other development pressures, as at Manassas, Gettysburg, and Antietam.

The battle between a developer and preservationists over part of Manassas began in 1988. It resulted in a massive federal government payoff to the developer of over $250,000 per acre for a 542-acre site. It also led to the creation of government organizations, notably the Civil War Sites Advisory Commission in Congress and the American Battlefield Protection Program in the Department of the Interior. A National Trust trustee was asked to establish a private, nonprofit organization to work with these two government entities. The Civil War Trust works to raise money and to negotiate and mediate with interested parties over conflicts at Civil War sites.[3]

There are also state organizations, such as the Kentucky Heritage Council and the Maryland Civil War Heritage Commission, and a plethora of local organizations and Civil War buffs and boosters. The town of Vicksburg, for example, has become quite taken over by preservation programs that interpret its Civil War siege. Visitors take a tour that follows the path of the victorious Union Army. They start on the plain above the city and pass by monuments to the soldiers of different states as they proceed closer to their goal.

While Vicksburg is dedicated to interpreting one Civil War battle of key importance, Fredericksburg, Virginia, looks at a complex layering of military and political history. This layering attracts tourists, but may also befuddle them as they find themselves tangled in the history of different periods. They are in the eighteenth century when they visit Washington's childhood home. They are in the early nineteenth century when they tour President James Madison's home, Montpelier. And they are in the mid-nineteenth century when on the Fredericksburg battlefields, where over seventeen thousand men died and eighty thousand were wounded in the course of four battles. Fredericksburg and Stafford County, Virginia, offer more military history for the tourist dollar than most competing sites; they invite tourists to "Walk in Washington's footsteps, Stand where brave men fell." They offer not just homes and battlefields with costumed interpreters, but also several museums where tourists can focus on another mode of recontextualization, namely the war relic removed from its surround and re-presented as exhibited object.

The Exhibited Object

Surplus military objects, including navy pea jackets and army fatigues, from earlier periods are recycled as fashion objects. Souvenirs of war, both guns and booty, are privately squirreled away in many British and American homes. But many other objects are difficult to integrate into everyday life. B-1 bombers, howitzers, and modern rockets have become the nucleus around which specialized museums have been built.

Soldiers have traditionally picked up souvenirs of war and

brought them home. Curators have become booty hunters at one remove. With an eye to the future, they must scavenge for cultural capital as soon as the battle is over and while the pickings are still good.

In the Smithsonian collection of minor artifacts from the Gulf War, one bit of booty is a small package of cookies. The sand-colored cookies are wrapped in cellophane and printed with the bakery's name and town: Amman, Jordan. They were found by one Captain Roberts of the Medical Reserve Corps as he toured Saudi Arabia and Kuwait in the immediate postwar days and took photographs and collected souvenirs.

To an earlier generation of soldiers and curators, the cookies would not have been seen as a collectible, much less a museum piece. But they now speak to the modern museum sensibility, as influenced by the new social history. The cookies are a telling, if somewhat maudlin, detail. They are meant to remind audiences that war is as much or more about people in peril as it is about guns in action. Possibly coming from the pocket of a young draftee, the cookies also speak to the effort to counter elitism in exhibits, to provide the common touch. This anti-elitism is reflected in other exhibits. As the Smithsonian's curator for military history said, "If you had come into this museum in 1960, it was essentially a white, elitist story." To remedy this, the museum tries to present uniforms of the lower ranks as well as the generals. From the Gulf War, it will also display the field jacket worn by Barbara Bush. "It's just regular issue. Just plain, right out of the stockroom."[4]

Britain's National Army Museum also has an exhibit of soldier's artifacts labeled "The Gulf War 1990–1991: Aftermath of a Battle." Contained in the glass cases are such articles as plastic cups, plates, and cutlery, a 'Blackadder' badge from the Logistic Support units who lived in a camp nicknamed Blackadder in the Saudi port of Al Jubayl, and a tinned 'Compo' ration. These artifacts emphasize the National Army Museum's mission of focusing on the fighting men and women. In accomplishing that mission, even plastic plates now become prize possessions.

Anticipating future needs, curators develop mental shopping lists during conflicts such as the Gulf War, deciding what will be of importance to future generations. A curator at the National Air and Space Museum hoped to acquire Scud and Patriot missiles, while the curator at the Air Force Museum was quoted as saying it would be "really nice" to have an A-10 for the collection. He also expressed interest in acquiring an Iraqi tank hit by a Maverick missile, but short of a total wreck. Such a casualty of war would show "This is what we did to them." What we did to the men inside can only be conjectured.[5]

Museum possession of another nation's property has increasingly become the object of contestation: the Elgin Marbles are the best-known example. Unlike these symbols of Greek antiquity and nationhood, there does not seem to be much demand for the return of captured fighter aircraft or armaments, at least, not as cultural objects. Much of the technology of wars past appears to be safely tucked away into major museums such as the Imperial War Museum (IWM) in London, and the National Air and Space Museum in Washington, D.C., two of the most important and the most popular.

The Imperial War Museum was founded by the British government in 1917. Its original purpose was to display material relating to World War I. Officially opened by King George V in the Crystal Palace in 1920, it later relocated to two galleries adjoining the former Imperial Institute in South Kensington before moving again in 1936 to its present location on the South Bank. In 1986 a major redevelopment scheme was undertaken. With the first phase now complete, the Imperial War Museum is flying the banner of the "*New* Imperial War Museum" and proudly displays several important design awards in the main exhibit hall.

Since its founding, the IWM's mission has broadened to include all of modern war, "the human story of war in the twentieth century." The emphasis is definitely on World War I and World War II. The main gallery space on the lower level is dedicated to the explanation and interpretation of the two wars. A series of small rooms explain these two major engagements with clarity and a minimum of political polemics. Several innovative exhibits attempt to give visitors a taste of what it was like. For World War I, a walk-through recreation of a 1916 trench on the Somme allows visitors to experience "what it was like to be a Tommy in the trenches." For World

War II, the "Blitz Experience" re-creates an air-raid shelter, complete with the jolt of a near miss and a tour of a blitzed street of 1940.

Center stage is occupied by the three-story exhibit gallery with its range of military weaponry, including, for example, the VI flying bomb and the V2 rocket, an M4 Sherman tank, a British 9.2 howitzer, a Zeppelin gondola, a Spitfire, a Daimler armored car, and a Polaris missile.

The IWM also has large outdoor exhibits at other sites. The cruiser HMS Belfast is moored on the Thames as an example of the Royal Navy's big gun ships. Over 120 aircraft, plus armored vehicles, midget submarines, and a 9.2-inch coastal gun are on exhibit at Duxford airfield, near Cambridge. Back in London, the Cabinet War Rooms are now open to tourists. Within the twenty-one-room complex, visitors can view the Cabinet Room, the Map Room, and the Prime Minister's Room, from which Churchill made a number of his radio broadcasts to the British people. A totally separate enterprise, the "Winston Churchill's Britain at War Theme Museum" invites visitors in four languages to relive the Blitz with "amazing realistic effects."

There is no institution clearly comparable to the Imperial War Museum on the other side of the Atlantic. One would have to combine the military history exhibits at the Smithsonian National Museum of American History with the vastly popular National Air and Space Museum.

In contrast to the "New" Imperial War Museum, with its very modern presentations, the military exhibits in the National Museum of American History are housed in dark rooms with an old-fashioned air. A prominent position near the entrance is reserved for George Washington's stuffed horse. There are the expected arrays of swords and pistols under glass and Civil War cannons. Tourists walks through the wreck of an old boat, without seeming to know why, and appear neither excited nor moved by the experience.

The new social history emphasizing gender, class, and race, so evident in other Smithsonian exhibits, is only minimally evident here. This is history waiting to be rewritten. In time, and given funds, it probably will be.

By contrast to the old-fashioned exhibits at the National

Museum of American History, those across the mall at the National Air and Space Museum are all glitz and glamour. A huge mural at the museum's entrance invites visitors to share the adventure of space exploration. Prominent display of the American flag makes the point that this has been preeminently an American adventure. The building itself is open and airy, like a huge modern aircraft terminal. In some sense, that is what it is. Aircraft from Orville and Wilbur Wright's to Lindbergh's to the most advanced rocketry hang suspended from the ceiling or poised to pierce through it. Bulky commercial airliners from the golden age of aircraft occupy another area of the hanger qua museum. Side galleries provide room to explore side issues, whether these be the role of women and African-Americans in flight or the scientific composition and characteristics of space itself.

Despite all the popular and political romance, conquest of space has not been entirely a success story. The most recent tragedy was the explosion of the Challenger rocket and the death of its crew, including its civilian member. This event is commemorated on a placard in the main hall. Another tragedy was the dropping of hydrogen bombs on Hiroshima and Nagasaki. Until recently, the only exhibit referring to this event has been a black-and-white film on the history of bombing in the twentieth century. Showing on a small screen in one of the side galleries, the film runs for approximately three minutes. When the mushroom cloud appears, the tape is silent. People who know what it is will know; those who do not, will not.

How much people can be expected to know is an important question in curatorship and interpretation. It was one of several issues involved in the controversy over how to present the Enola Gay, the plane that dropped the hydrogen bomb on Hiroshima. Curators initially wanted a text that provided a full social context and that questioned the necessity of dropping the bomb for ending the war. Veterans groups were angered by this and by language they considered leftist in tone and political motivation, such as the description of the Pacific war as a "war of vengeance." Under pressure, the Smithsonian revised the text, which, in turn, angered historians who disagreed with the veterans.

Difficulties in interpretation occur in all recontextualizations. Some pervasive difficulties with war representations can be singled out as deserving of special consideration. These are as follows.

Issues in Interpretation

Technology versus Social History

A tension exists between the desire to display the technology of war and the desire to create a narrative relating the social history of the war period. The largest museums, such as the IWM, may attempt both. Other museums, with more limited space and/or resources, often choose to emphasize one or the other.

The Intrepid Sea-Air-Space Museum, located on the Intrepid aircraft carrier at a New York City pier, is a good example of a museum devoted mainly to war technology. Over forty aircraft are displayed on the flight deck, including a Lockheed A-12 Blackbird, reportedly the fastest and highest flying secret plane. Both a Growler submarine and an Edson destroyer are moored alongside the Intrepid. Inside the carrier there are many smaller exhibits on military engagements extending up to and including the Gulf War. Interpretation is kept to a minimum, and few guides are in evidence. The whole floating exhibit is designed to honor veterans and to show that "freedom is never free." As one columnist wrote, "The Intrepid takes you back to boom-boom, John Wayne, and simple values that, when all is said and done, have kept the United States kicking like a colt for almost 216 years."[6]

A different motive underlies the exhibit created by the Cincinnati Historical Society and called "Cincinnati at War." The staff of the society were influenced by three factors: the then upcoming fiftieth anniversary of American participation in World War II, the opening of the society's new home in the recently restored Union Terminal (whose busiest years had been the war years), and the opportunity it provided to involve Cincinnatians who had lived through the war years. The tone of the souvenir booklet was remarkably different from the buoyant patriotism of the Intrepid. It is summed up in the statement, "The Historical Society wanted to present a view of the war that would commemorate, rather than celebrate, the commitment, ingenuity, sacrifice, and courage of Americans on the home front as well as the battlefield." The statement of purpose concluded with, "The sixty million wartime deaths do not allow a celebration."[7]

True to its goal, the exhibit shows every feature of home front activity: rationing, scrapping, selling war bonds, cultivating victory gardens, and knitting, among them. The entrance of large numbers of women into factory work is shown, and mention is made of the discrimination encountered by women, blacks, and Appalachian migrants in industry. The exhibit also doesn't shy away from racism in the armed forces or from the subject of Japanese-American internment. Some of the latter group were relocated to Cincinnati, and their stories are told.

The Cincinnati exhibit gives heroism its due in providing the stories of local men and women who served in different capacities, and in relating the joy of victory and the tragedy of deaths in the line of duty. Union Terminal, with its impressive Art Deco murals, dome, and overall retro appearance, provides a unique and evocative frame for this interpretation of Cincinnati during the war years.

Intrinsic Limits to Interpretation

Industrial sites pose intrinsic problems to interpretation; war sites and exhibits pose problems that may seem even more daunting. Realistically, one cannot have a certain percentage of tourists maimed and killed in the name of authenticity, much as this may seem an attractive option to residents of towns such as Vicksburg that are overrun by this invading army.

Civil war battles are periodically re-created and reenacted in both the United States and Great Britain, between North and South, Roundhead and Cavalier. Each of these wars offered cunning strategies, valiant charges, and man-to-man combat complimented by horses and cannon. Reenacted battles allow for the display of bravery, sometimes splendid, sometimes mediocre, playacting. Tourists know the South shall rise again the next day, including those weekend warriors lying dead in battle.

The actors engaged in these mock battles are themselves

tourists of a kind. People engaged in each activity—as mock combatants or spectators—are attempting to experience or relive the past. The tourists get to be generals, above the fray. They hold the high ground and survey the battlefields spread before them. This time, however, there are maps to explain which regiment is where and who will win in the end. Tourists have both knowledge and power, secure in a peaceful rolling landscape whose "viewshed" (as preservationist jargon calls the surrounding landscape) has been protected by federal order and payoffs to developers. No high-rise condominiums, much less a surprise rebel attack, will disturb their reverie.

This quiet is one of the strangest and most incongruous points about old battlefields. They are silent as cemeteries because they *are* cemeteries. They are religious ground, consecrated in blood. Real battles are, of course, just the opposite—filled with a terrifying cacophony. Interpretive films shown at sites attempt to provide the sounds of battle and conflict. At Harper's Ferry, the visitor gets to put together the pieces: the evocative natural site, the preserved ruins of the Civil War town whose arsenal John Brown seized, the film, exhibits, and costumed interpreters portraying soldiers and towns people.

Videos are a frequent aid to interpretation in war museums and outdoor sites. The visitor presses part of the screen that indicates the piece of technology he or she wants to see demonstrated. The tape then shows how the weapon worked, while the actual weapon stands as silent as sculpture.

Special exhibits try to make up for what these silent, sterile displays lack. The "Blitz Experience" at the IWM crowds about twenty people into what is supposed to be an underground air-raid shelter. They then listen to a tape, supposedly of Londoners who are sharing the shelter with them. The final message of the Londoners, "We're all in this together, Harry," seems the appropriate ending to a situation comedy peopled by resilient Cockneys, the original Eastenders.

The Blitz Experience includes mild use of smells. The stench coming from the IWM's Trench Experience is evident even before the visitor enters this walk-through exhibit. The Trench Experience also has the rat-a-tat-tat of artillery overhead and voices of soldiers. The smell from the Trench Experience is, in fact, the only direct assault the tourist will experience in the whole museum.

Even as curators strive to provide a suggestion of what war was like, it can only be the mildest suggestion. A former British Army officer, after visiting the IWM, commented that what he missed in the interpretation was the sheer *physicality* of operation. "They don't show what happens when you load a heavy artillery gun . . . that has to get filled with powder, that has to have its charge calculated, be lifted and shoved in. . . . And sometimes the charge explodes and blows up the gun and everybody with it." Even videos effectively filter the physicality and never show the technology going wrong, which would send the wrong message about both technology and the society that produced it. But what messages are being sent? For this, we need turn to more extrinsic considerations conditioning the act of interpretation.

Extrinsic Political Pressures

Wars are times when the extraordinary call on citizens for sacrifice must be justified in terms of higher social, economic, and political ends. As such, wars provide excellent material for cultural narratives. Such narratives range from those told by old boys to impress the women and each other, to the narratives told by media makers such as television and movie producers, to those told by politicians hoping to cast their country's actions in the best possible light, while furthering their own careers.

Paul Aragon once wrote that myth is the conveyer belt of consciousness. If so, war represents an important position along the belt's course, a place where notions of national strength or weakness, honor or dishonor, bravery or cowardice, are added or subtracted. For many decades, Americans were told that their nation had never lost a war. Then came Vietnam, and they were no longer so sure. The resulting ambivalence has been represented in a range of films that differ significantly from World War II films and from what Studs Terkel has described as the myth of the "good war."[8] Whatever Vietnam was, it was not a good war. Among other things, it was hard to translate into a convincing narrative, and the nation remained divided and confused as to why we were there and whether we should be there.

Vietnam was repeatedly referred to in the months leading up to, during, and after the Gulf War. This suggests that historical consciousness is not dead in our society, even if it is selective. But collective memory has always had its lapses and points of emphasis. What is increasingly important, however, is the role of the media in shaping this historical consciousness, a process evident in its repeated Vietnam–Gulf War comparisons.

Despite modern cynicism, wars remain national testing grounds. Revisionist historians now tell us that the narratives spun around the Battle of Britain exaggerated the social solidarity and willing sacrifice that occurred, while underemphasizing profiteering, thievery, and a simple reluctance to share in a time of danger and shortages. Terkel's book similarly recounts considerable profiteering on the American side. But this is not the narrative that most residents of either nation want to hear, and certainly not those residents who lived through World War II. The brave soldier at the battle front and Mrs. Miniver at the home front still dominate both the media and popular consciousness.

Historical representations provide vehicles for interpreting war and nation to the public. As such, they are subject to external pressures from a range of sources. Curators may share dominant political interpretations, or may experience an interpretation as alien. In either case, the curators' jobs may depend on how well they negotiate the distance between past and present political realities.

For example, the reunification of Germany has brought to the fore questions about the interpretation of concentration camps, including Buchenwald, in East Germany. The camp had been administered by loyal Communists, who were later accused of deliberately and dramatically reshaping history to suit their own ideological purposes. Special displays were erected to the glory of the German Communists who died at this Nazi camp. But little mention was made of the sufferings and sacrifice of Jews, and none of gypsies and homosexuals also interned. As a result of public pressure, the local government administering Buchenwald appointed a new director, a thirty-six-year-old historian with a specialization in concentration camps, notably Buchenwald. He promised a more historically complete and sensitive interpretation. "Truth and memory are fundamental to our mission here." But when it was shortly revealed that he, too, had been a Communist Party member, he was forced to resign. His political credentials, not his professional credentials, were called into question by the heightened political pressures created by the recent empowerment of groups that had formerly been silenced.[9]

Curators in Britain and the States are aware of such pressures. External pressures can be exerted by local, state, and federal governments, as well as by organized interest groups and publics. Congressional involvement in the planning of Washington's National Air and Space Museum was one reason behind the positive presentations on weaponry and other examples of aviation technology.[10] Local and state museums often exhibit boosterism, featuring shows focusing on local sacrifices and contributions to the war effort.

The public also gets involved in using historic representations to rewrite history, or at least to present their particular interpretation of it. In the spring of 1991 and following upon pressure from organized Indian groups, Congress authorized changing the name of Custer National Battlefield Park to Little Bighorn Park. Congress also authorized erecting a monument to the fallen Indians, estimated to number 6 Cheyenne and 24 Sioux, to stand alongside the memorial to the 224 massacred soldiers. The congressman who championed the campaign, Ben Nighthorn Campbell, remarked that the battlefield had been "the only one battlefield in the world named after the loser and the only USA National Park named after an individual." But Custer's surviving relatives didn't see it that way, especially one Colonel George Armstrong Custer III, who said, "I'm just kind of wiped out . . . after all of this," and commented that Congress had not invited any opposition to the change at the hearing. "Five members of the Custer family died in the battle—so we earned the named Custer battlefield right there." He complained to the press, "I thought this was supposed to be a democracy."[11]

Custer lost the actual battle; now his descendants have lost the symbolic battle, at least for the time being. The problem is not whether or not America is a democracy, but how to balance competing claims within a pluralistic society. This is especially the case when formerly silenced groups, such as Indian constituencies, rightly demand recognition and empowerment and rebel against the "symbolic violence" of commemorating only white losses.

Women represent another major category seeking to escape symbolic violence and symbolic annihilation, that is, having their participation and contribution simply erased from the public record.[12] In the past several decades, social historians have begun to give serious recognition to the activities of women during wartime, both in active service and at the home front. This shift of attention is slowly replacing an emphasis once restricted to great generals, great battles, and the sacrifice of soldiers.

Even so, conflicts emerge regarding the participation of women in historic representations. In 1991, a woman sued the National Park Service for not allowing her to enact the role of a soldier in historic representations staged at Antietam battlefield. These historic representations are not battle reenactments, but merely marching and firing drills. Lauren Cook trained to play the fife and studied military tactics as a member of the 21st Georgia volunteer infantry and two other Civil War organizations. "I think I do a far better job than a lot of the men out there," she told the press.[13] The park superintendent did not believe these activities were appropriate for women. He emphasized instead that scheduled events did include roles for women, "including rolling bandages, trying to find a loved one on the battlefield or portraying Clara Barton, founder of the American Red Cross, who served in the battle."

What is particularly interesting is that historians estimate that there *were* approximately four hundred women soldiers among the three million soldiers who served either the Union or Rebel cause. Ms. Cook argues that documents show that at least two women fought at Antietam, disguising themselves as she disguises herself for the reenactment. None of this fit the superintendent's view of history. "We have a very strict standards here . . . and I don't apologize for it."

It may be a strict standard, but stricter than history, which is often less simple than the textbooks record. Or it may be an inappropriate standard, given the wider goals of many historic representations. These goals may include giving all members of society a chance not just to learn the narrative, but to become part of the narrative. Historic sites can provide places for social healing. This is especially true of battlefields, the evident reason why François Mitterand met and shook the hand of Helmut Kohl at Verdun, and why Reagan went to Normandy, and why there was a proposal floated for exchange visits of American and Japanese heads of state to Pearl Harbor and Hiroshima.

Education versus Entertainment

Curators recognize the tension between education and entertainment. As Alan Borg, director-general of the Imperial War Museum has written, "The prime role of the museum is educational, but we also know that you cannot educate anyone if you are dull and boring. For this reason," he continues, "we have tried to make the new Imperial War Museum as lively and informative as possible." Borg and his associates also want to communicate a balanced view of the complex phenomenon called modern war, covering "controversial and unpleasant topics" as well as those reflecting heroism and glory.[14]

Curators, architects, and planners involved in the restoration of the Historic Dockyard at Chatham were also aware of this dilemma. The massive dockyard complex, parts of which dated back to the seventeenth century, could be seen as a hard sell. To make this riverside complex more exciting, preservationists introduced a range of animated figures and other special effects in the main exhibits. Tourists follow the path of a new apprentice during the dockyard's Georgian heyday, thereby learning about the yard's social organization and all the crafts that go into constructing a warship. Among the figures they encounter are an animated rat and rat catcher, as well as a man caught with his pants quite literally down. If this isn't entertaining enough, a full schedule of special events complements the permanent exhibits. In 1992 these events included a traditional boat festival on the river Medway, a flower festival, a model railway exhibition, heavy horse day and several jumble sale events, and also a production of the *Pirates of Penzance* in the dockyard church and a mad hatter's tea party in the Commissioner's Garden. Such a wide range of events, some with a tenuous connection to dockyard history, others with no connection whatsoever, would make preservation purists livid. But such events, as well as providing both a social center and source of income for the local people, popularize a site that many otherwise might find dull and inaccessible.

The juxtaposition between lived history and the visitor's experience of its sites and/or mementos can be striking. Battlefields such as Verdun were sites of tremendously high levels of human destruction and tend to be interpreted with restraint and reverence. Yet today's visitor is provided with reassuring directions on "getting there, where to eat, and accommodations," whereas yesterday's soldier had only the trenches. Tourists come freely; soldiers came under military orders.

How accurate can the portrayal of war be? Schoolchildren represent a large proportion of the audience. Would a stronger Blitz Experience give them nightmares? Would the National Air and Space Museum be as popular if it presented both sides of war? Would civil war battlefields provide for nice family outings if they were not such pleasing landscapes? While curators and critics debate how far they can go in the direction of education and accuracy, there are several social forces pushing them in the direction of inaccuracy and entertainment.

First, there is the *romance of war* itself. Imaginations are fired by daring generals and admiring ladies, regiments in full dress uniforms, tender meetings and partings. All this is ready fodder for historic representations. Safe from the scene of battle, London's Apsley House and Wellington Museum celebrated "Waterloo Week." The entertainment began with a Victorian soiree featuring a chamber orchestra and finger buffet. Two lunchtime concerts followed, and in the evenings visitors were invited to performances of *Wellington,* a play emphasizing the general's friendship with Lady Mary Sackville West. In addition, the Waterloo Assembly, with its thirty plus costumed participants, revived the quadrilles written for Wellington's balls in 1815, along with other period dances. All in all, Waterloo Week promised great fun and lots of romance.

In the American South, the Civil War conjures up romantic images of Southern belles and Confederate officers, though not necessarily to the minds of African-Americans. Such images owe much to the enduring popularity of *Gone With the Wind*. As setting for this romance, Atlanta profits directly. But other Southern cities, such as Natchez and Memphis, also host historic representations and tourist events designed to derive profit from such mythic images.

More to a man's taste, perhaps, is the *romance of technology*. The big machinery of war dominates exhibits through size alone. There is also the thrill of seeing dangerous armaments about which one has heard or read. Survivors of the Blitz get to see the VI and V2: "So that's what they were dropping on us," said one visitor at the IWM. Walking into a large exhibit hall is like walking into an automobile showroom filled with impressive makes and models, each capable of performing an impressive set of tasks. The North American B-51 Mustang fighter was "capable of escorting the bombers of the United States Air Force to Berlin and back," and made "a crucial contribution to the battle for air supremacy over Germany." The German radial-engine FW190 was "one of the fastest and most maneuverable fighters of the war." Modern technology creates its own ideology and justification, more enduring that the great ideological divisions that separated the Axis and Allies.[15] In the context of the international arms market, such exhibits are showrooms of vintage models. For the latest advances, one goes direct to the dealers.

A third force encouraging more entertaining representations is the *competition from the entertainment media*. War is a staple of film and television. Consciously or unconsciously, historic representations hoping to widen their audience adopt the media's promotional discourse. The Cabinet War Rooms are advertised as follows: "The last defence of the British war effort is a 3 foot slab of concrete"—a dramatic introduction to the Cabinet War Rooms, which are a relatively small complex of offices, hallways, and conference rooms.

Besides providing a highly dramatic discourse, which the history industry mimics, the mass media bombards the public with war images. Death, destruction, and human tragedy of every form have become regular items on the nightly news, as well as on dramas and documentaries. The public becomes increasingly inured to such images. Still photographs that would horrify, as in the IWM exhibit on Belsen, are images we have already seen and that have lost some of their initial impact. Exhibits must be strong enough to have an effect, but not so strong that they scare away the audience.

Historic Representations as Art and as Kitsch

Art has traditionally provided one conduit for socially sublimating the horror of war, raising it to another level at which it can be appreciated with distance and dispassion. The IWM has several galleries devoted to art depicting World Wars I and II. But perhaps the most effective is a gallery devoted to David Smith's surrealistic "Medals of Dishonor," which communicates a distinctly modern and anti-war sensibility that balances in some measure the romance of technology played out in the main exhibit hall.

Like historic representations, art is open to interpretation. This means it is also open to politics, as the long-raging debate over Maya Lin's Vietnam memorial indicates. Once degraded as "a black gash of shame," it has become the nation's most visited memorial, even as several more traditional statues have been located nearby. The function of these traditional sculptures appears to placate those opposed to modern design, which is implicitly more open to interpretation than images of brave men of action.

Historic representations have often arranged objects of war into aesthetically pleasing displays, as if they were sea shells or pressed flowers. Whole rooms at Culzean and Warwick castles are filled with sword displays, with the pretty patterns belying the bloody purpose. Uniforms also have been appreciated for their aesthetic appeal. The costume gallery at Britain's National Army Museum is reportedly a favorite haunt of fashion students.

War representations can also take on the quality of kitsch. The Intrepid Museum has a bizarre plastic model of Franklin Delano Roosevelt reading the paper. The National Army Museum displays the skeleton of Napoleon's horse. Private collections of regimental insignia, bits of uniforms, weaponry, are all forms of kitsch. When art critic Sir Nicolas Pevsner defined kitsch as that which is overly sweet and sentimental, lacking in taste, he may have been thinking more of feminine kitsch. Male kitsch is also sentimental if not necessarily sweet in the same sense—a re-imagining of periods of male glory and comradeship, alongside of which much of civilian life pales by comparison. Nazi uniforms represent forbidden power to punks whose real sources of power are limited and short lived.

War can also provide for an aesthetic of the grotesque. Grotesque art involves "the sense that, though our attention has been arrested, our understanding is unsatisfied."[16] For Thomas Mann the grotesque is "something more than the truth, something real in the extreme, not something arbitrary, false, absurd, and contrary to reality."[17] Visiting the Holocaust Memorial Museum, journalist Philip Gourevitch was struck by how the sheer horror of the exhibits created a sense of excitement, and seduced visitors into the role of voyeurs of the prurient. Among many other examples of the grotesque aesthetic was a video playing and replaying footage of killing squads in action. Observing this footage, Gourevitch felt as though he were watching a peep show or snuff film. Among a crowd of tourists glued to the screen, he watched successive images including "naked people standing about to be killed, naked people lying down dead. Close-up of a woman's face and throat as a knife is plunged into her breast—blood all over. Someone holds a severed head in his hand. Mass graves of thousands. . . . Naked women dragged to death. Shooting. Screaming. Blackout. The film begins again."[18]

The question becomes to what extent the presentation of the grotesque helps construct the historical narrative and to what extent it warps the historical encounter, leading more toward titillation than serious reflection.[19] As with the other issues in the interpretation of war, fine lines must be walked, and pressures come from all sides. Yet in perhaps no other area does commemoration play so important a role. It helps society deal with its sense of loss, its sense of guilt or honor. It helps it find and maintain a sense of direction.

None of these exhibits, however, are neutral acts. None are free from political pressures or, indeed, from any of the conflicts characteristic of modern society. Finding a sense of national direction from historic representations is no easy task and is usually a matter of more intellectual complexity and subtlety than such exhibits—aimed at attracting a wide audience and pleasing a plurality of interests—can or will allow.

A Green
and Pleasant Land

The grandeur of the medieval past at Bodiam Castle, Sussex

English Country Houses

Ickworth House, Suffolk

Saltram Park, Plymouth

The English Landscape Garden, as seen at Stourhead, Wiltshire

Nostalgia for the Agrarian Past

Old Sturbridge Village, Massachusetts, street scene

Through the garden arch

The New England village, as seen at Litchfield, Connecticut

Historic Deerfield, Massachusetts

The Industrial Ruin in the Landscape

The charcoal shed and furnace at Bonawe Furnace,
Taynuilt, near Oban, Scotland

The industrial shell, transformed by adaptive reuse

Apartments and offices in Lowell, Massachusetts

The consumption of history at historic hotels such as
the DonCeSar Beach Resort and Spa, St. Petersburg Beach, Florida

The history of consumption, represented by "The Big Duck,"
former poultry products store now historic and architectural landmark,
Flanders, Long Island, New York

Major sites of world importance, such as the Georgian city of Bath, England, are exposed to dangers and opportunities created by massive tourism

Religious Preservation in Secular Society

CHAPTER 6

HOLY GHOST CHURCH RESTORED IN HAWAII
"This is more than a church project," says
Merideth Ching (a financial backer). "This is
a gathering place for the whole community."
—Historic Preservation News,
November 1992

A re we becoming a more secular society? While some new forms of worship and belief are on the rise, churches, synagogues, and cathedrals with declining congregations or altogether empty stand witness to the declining authority of other, older religions.[1] These structures are now the object of preservation campaigns. What is especially interesting is how these campaigns are waged not in the name of religion, but in the name of community, or even society. Preservationists argue that the religious edifice can serve an old end in a new manner. They bypass all specific issues of faith and doctrine—issues that would be divisive and restrict the sources of financial support—to cut to a new heart of the matter. In so doing, they lend support to the sociological notion that religions exist not to serve God, but to foster moral communities. Both the work involved in preserving religious edifices as well as the final result are seen by some preservationists involved as creating a new basis for moral order.[2] This is especially the case in the United States. In Britain, the architecture itself is treated with near-sacred reverence and respect. Even so, social and moral issues arise as preservationists attempt to save religious structures in an increasingly secular society.

Viewed historically, secularization is related to the rise of modern capitalism, the modern state, and modern science. All three social forces weakened the hold of religion over people's minds and behavior. Secularization has had two major impacts on modern society. First, religious beliefs have become increasingly subjective and open to choice, as people became increasingly free to explore alternative explanations and meaning systems, rather than being forced to obey one, ruling belief system. Secondly, institutionalized religion has become depoliticized in the sense that it no longer serves to order and interpret society.[3] Any remaining ties between church and state tend to be inspirational and/or ceremonial, rather than all-powerful and determining.

Speculating on possible responses to secularization, Daniel Bell has spoken of the rise of "redemptive religions," especially among the intellectual and professional classes. For Bell, the ruptures and excesses of the modern age might lead some people to search for the continuity that comes from tradition. They would then freely accept the past, "in order to maintain the continuity of moral meanings."[4] Their actions would be redemptive to the extent that these people see themselves and are seen as discharging their sense of obligations to "the moral imperatives of the community."[5]

This search for meaning and redemption could not occur in a vacuum. Rather, *mediating institutions,* located in between the central government and the individual, can be seen as providing a locus for the fulfillment of moral obligations. These institutions include the family, church, neighborhood, and voluntary associations. Through their mediating role, the self is able to create itself through social processes, as the individual existence is balanced by an existence associated with a greater humanity.

In the United States and, to a more limited extent, in Great

Britain, historic preservation is increasingly assuming the appearance and role of a mediating institution. Historic preservation provides a set of values and activities. It provides a locus for caring and a means of creating the self through social process as devotees go about their chosen work of "saving" buildings and creating a moral community.

▓ *Religious Preservation in the United States*

The moral purpose and mediating role of preservation in general is most visible in the particular context of religious preservation. This much is evident in the names that preservation organizations have chosen for themselves and their activities, names such as Inspired Partnerships, Sacred Trusts, and Common Bond, and, in Britain, SAVE Our National Heritage, among other names. The purpose of the organizations is to restore and protect significant religious properties, with significance defined as the importance of the architecture or the property's role in community history. Sometimes there is still an active congregation; in other situations the structure has been virtually or completely abandoned.

Church organizations can be but are not always the preservationist's ally in the fight to preserve religious properties. Sometimes the church organization is the enemy and would like very much to tear the structure down in favor of parking spaces or a more modern and profitable edifice. In such instances, preservationists must find a firmer, broader source of legitimation. What often emerges is a shared appreciation of the religious structure's importance as a social and cultural marker, a sacred site for community memory. The theme for the umbrella organization Inspired Partnership's fourth national conference summed up this goal: "Reinvesting in Religious Buildings to Benefit American Communities." The conference program elaborated upon this goal. "Older religious properties and their congregations are the cornerstones of many communities. Today, perhaps more than ever, they are a steady force amid rapid changes that might otherwise threaten neighborhood stability. Sacred buildings are vital centers of spiritual comfort and neighborhood services. And they are often architectural wonders that foster a special sense of place for passersby and congregants alike."

While the legitimation is based on communion within the neighborhood, and spanning past and present, the conference program reveals how this redemptive pursuit to save religious structures is based on the activities of the professional classes, much as Bell might have predicted. Specific sessions included "The ABCs of a Capital Campaign," "Publicity How-To: Keeping the Public Eye on Your Campaign," and "Tapping the Congregation: How to Maximize Member Giving for Capital Improvements." The preservationist appears as much a manager as a cultural leader.

At preservation conferences, professionalism mixes easily with high moral purpose. Professions by their nature tend to claim the high moral ground to provide themselves with a sense of purpose and to garner broad social legitimation.[6] Professional meetings assume the quality of class reunions *and* religious revivals, as members meet to renew their common bond and to become reinspired by the shared moral goal.

If preservationists see themselves as leaders active in a moral cause, their campaigns frequently take the form of crusades. Campaigns seek to "save" buildings from disgrace, demolition, and ruin. Religious structures play a specially significant part in the collective memory as places where moments in personal history become part of the flow of collective history. This collective history transcends individual experiences and lifetimes. One of the proponents for the rescue of Chicago's St. Mary of the Angels recalled how he and his five siblings had been baptized, confirmed, schooled, and married in the church. "St. Mary's is very important to the community. . . . It's part of the reason people buy property here. If it goes, the neighborhood will suffer."[7]

Religious preservation is not always a means of maintaining community. Sometimes, it is a means of restoring community. A couple who had recently bought a vacation home in the resort town of Tupper Lake, new York, found that the local synagogue, built in 1906, had been closed since 1959. The wife began a preservation campaign that involved descendants of the earlier congregation. One eighty-year-old woman wrote personal letters to former residents, urging donations by recalling how the synagogue had figured in important events in their personal history.

Since there were few remaining Jewish residents in Tupper Lake, plans were made to turn the synagogue into a Jewish museum and to provide space for historical society exhibits. As contributors began asking when services would resume, however, the religious mission was reconsidered. As the eighty-year-old woman said, "The Jews will come in from out of the woods . . . they'll want to gather and talk and meet with each other." The preservation effort assumed a *Field of Dreams* quality: if we preserve it, they will come. It became not simply a task in fundraising and repair, but a "mitzvoth—a profound obligation, an inescapable burden, performed with a joyous heart."[8]

American religious preservation draws upon the American civil religion.[9] It exalts pluralism and readily calls up the immigrant religious experience and its importance to the making of the nation. As an editor of *Preservation News* wrote, "Our churches, many of which were built by immigrants to establish roots in this new country while retaining customs from their native lands, also represent a tradition of helping those in need regardless of their faith or race."[10]

In similar fashion, the argument for the preservation of a Chicago church was based on the idea that "Holy Family Church's real contribution is that it has served as the Ellis Island of the Midwest for wave after wave of immigrants, first the Irish, then the Germans, Italians, Slavs, Mexicans, and African-Americans. They have all claimed the church as their own."[11]

These campaigns reinforce another aspect of the American civil religion, namely voluntaryism. The idea of everyone pitching in for the common good reflects a Rousseauean image of society. But, then, it was Rousseau who coined the term "civil religion" in the first place. This voluntaristic and pluralistic emphasis is much less evident in Great Britain. There, campaigns for religious preservation appear more clearly as struggles among status groups with conflicting interests and agendas.

▨ *Religious Preservation in Britain: Overview*

A recent American visitor to Great Britain commented that the British must be a very religious people because they built so many churches. What she didn't realize is, first, that they had so many centuries in which to build them. Religious structures in Britain represent not simply the rock of ages but a historic lode from ages past, Celtic crosses and ruins, Roman, Saxon, medieval, Renaissance, and so on right up to the present. The Victorians, in their proselytizing zeal, particularly in urban areas, were responsible for many churches.[12]

The second point the American visitor missed is that many of these churches stand empty or underutilized. These are redundant churches, and they are a major problem for the Church of England and the dissenting sects.

In 1969 the Redundant Churches Fund was established with the purpose of preserving the redundant churches or parts of churches belonging to the Church of England. To be preserved, churches had to have some claim to historic or archaeological interest or architectural quality.

Such properties became legally vested in the Fund through one of two schemes laid out in the Pastoral Measure of 1983, which was passed by the General Synod of the Church of England, ratified by Parliament, and received the Royal Assent. Under this measure, which replaced one passed in 1969, application and qualification procedures usually take less than one year, thus minimizing further damage and the costliness of repairs if undertaken.

Once a church is officially declared redundant, all worship ceases and it becomes the financial and legal responsibility of the Fund. Over a period of several years, the Fund assesses the church's merit and significance and tries to find a suitable alternate use. If none is found, the Fund can either restore and maintain the church "in retirement," or demolish it. By the end of 1992, 694 churches had undergone adaptive reuse, while approximately equal numbers had been restored or demolished (281 and 292 respectively). Seventy-four had other outcomes, unspecified.[13]

Another four redundant churches have been preserved by the Historic Buildings and Monuments Commission, and English

Heritage includes many ancient religious structures and monuments among the total of 354 properties for which it is responsible. They range from the famous and frequently visited, such as Fountains Abbey (a World Heritage site, under joint control with the National Trust) and Lindesfarne Priory down to small Saxon churches.

English Heritage has been facing financial difficulties in carrying out its mandate and has already cut back staff. In 1992, its controversial Chairman Jocelyn Stevens proposed that certain properties then controlled by English Heritage should be purchased by either private owners or local authorities. The so-called "hit-list" included 203 properties, among them Westminster Chapter House and Avebury stone circle.

One of English Heritage's own subcommittees, the Ancient Monuments Advisory Committee, denounced the plan as contradicting the commission's statutory duty of preserving the monuments delegated to its care. Other groups involved in preservation, notably SAVE Britain's Heritage, the Council for the Protection of Rural England, the Council for British Archaeology, and the National Trust, all warned of the loss of government protection that would result from such a change in ownership.

Preservationists also objected to sites being evaluated not just for their historic importance, but also for their "development potential." To Marianne Watson-Smith, of SAVE, this new entrepreneurial attitude represented a thinly disguised form of cultural Darwinism: "This policy is appalling, mis-conceived, and ill thought out—taking the view that it is only the best of our heritage that matters, the survival of the fittest."[14]

To opponents, it was the duty of the government, replacing that of religion, to treat all ancient religious structures as sacred. But not all members of government, or even all members of English Heritage, agreed with this sentiment. Furthermore, the new entrepreneurialism spreading throughout museums and other cultural institutions will also increasingly affect what gets preserved and how it is presented to the public. As of this writing, procedures within English Heritage were still being established, and the implications for religious preservation remained to be seen.

One can, however, say that the role of both the Redundant Churches Fund and English Heritage reflects the more centralized structure of British preservation as a whole, compared to the localistic and voluntaryistic structure of American preservation, wherein organizations serve more as clearing houses of information rather than as the main determiners of what gets preserved.

National differences between Britain and the States can also be detected in responses to issues relating not simply to whether to preserve, but how to preserve. These issues are considered in the following section.

From Anti-scrape to Adaptive Reuse

In Britain, the biggest debate in nineteenth-century religious preservation involved what was known as the "anti-scrape" movement. Anti-Scrape was a philosophy of minimal maintenance and virtually no restoration of ancient structures. It was a reaction against what was seen as the overrestoration of sites such as Vezeley in France, which went far beyond preserving remaining physical evidence to create an image of what might have been. The anti-scrape philosophy was propounded by John Ruskin, William Morris, and the Society for the Protection of Ancient Buildings.

For Ruskin, the term "restoration" denoted "the most total destruction which a building can suffer." It was as impossible to restore great architecture as it was to raise the dead. "That spirit which is given only by the hand and eye of the workman can never be recalled." Better to let the past go gently to ruin, to view with awe the passage of time, and to meditate on what once was. "There was yet in the old some life, some mysterious suggestion of what it had been, and of what it had lost; some sweetness in the gentle lines which rain and sun had wrought."[15]

Ruskin would be appalled by the range of preservation strategies practiced today. Others, however, argue that buildings should be neither left to decline nor overrestored, "pickled in aspic" at some arbitrary time. Architectural critic Ada Louise Huxtable has argued that "a good old building should develop layers of aesthetic mean-

ing like the rings of a tree, continually enriched, rather than isolated, by contemporary functions."[16]

Some structures can be successfully restored to their original state and social purpose. Parish churches are forever mounting appeals for repairs or new roofs. And the great cathedrals
provide religious services even as unending maintenance continues. For the majority of structures, however, another social purpose must be found. The question becomes, which forms of adaptive
reuse are acceptable and appropriate, and which represent acts of
desecration?

David Lowenthal has argued that the British have greater
reservations than do Americans about seeing sacred properties
used for such secular purposes as private homes.[17] Based on my
research, I believe American preservationists have an implicit slid-
ing scale of appropriateness that affects their decisions about which
forms of adaptive reuse are right and which are not right.

At the top of the scale are those uses that retain the religious
function or that translate it into civil religion. Preservationists feel
they have done good work when an old church or synagogue
becomes home to a new congregation, when it serves the needs of
the homeless, or when it can be transformed into a community cultural center, house a historical society or art museum. Some social
or cultural purpose should be present. When it is present, preservation serves its own advocates redemptively. It is seen as rising
above narrow personal, and especially financial interests, and as providing a communal good.

Other acceptable uses serve more particular class interests. The
conversion of a Boston Unitarian Meetinghouse into an architect's
studio, and a New Haven church into a center for cardiologists, were
seen as acceptable adaptive reuses, while the conversion of an
Episcopal church in New York into a discotheque was considered
beyond the pale. This contrast derives, at least in part, from the
upper- to upper-middle-class status of architecture and cardiology
and also the valued services these professions provide. By contrast,
a discotheque seems a mere occasion for release, which can be found
in many forms and is not productive. Also, architects and cardiologists can usually be relied upon to behave in a reasonably controlled

manner, at least at work and in front of clients, again unlike crowds of discotheque habitués.

Thus within secular society there remains some appreciation of what is socially appropriate and morally right. Religious structures still have some sense of awe attached to them, even if almost everyone has forgotten the finer points of theology.

The issue of adaptive reuse is one manifestation of a larger tension between religious claims and economic needs. Two major controversies, one on each side of the Atlantic, reflect the tension between the sacred and the secular. In Britain, the question concerns the cost of maintaining cathedrals: whose responsibility is it? In America, the question relates to the politics of landmarking and who controls whether a church stands or is demolished.

Cathedrals as Money Changers

Cathedrals have a historic role as focal points for the religious and social life of their cities and surrounding regions.[18] People come as penitents, participants, and pilgrims, and increasingly as tourists. As a result, the cathedrals are wearing out.

Who should be responsible for the maintenance and restoration of Britain's magnificent cathedrals? Should it be the congregations? This would be an impossible task, especially given their shrinking numbers. Should the Church of England with be responsible? Church leaders point out that the annual budget only covers operating expenses, leaving little to contribute to the estimated 70 to 150 million pounds needed for cathedral repair and restoration. If the cathedrals truly are national treasures, should not the nation-state be financially responsible? But if it is, will the churches lose control of their own operations, and what will prevent the dead hand of state bureaucracy from adding other burdens? If the fund raising is left primarily to each cathedral's leadership, how far can or should it go in turning the cathedrals into profitable enterprises?

The mighty, if crumbling, cathedrals are among the most powerful of religious symbols. The different responses to their plight and the high-pitched level of the debate reveal continued uncertainty about the role of religion in secular society.

Different cathedrals have taken different tacks and found themselves facing different moral and financial dilemmas. Ely Cathedral has gone the furthest in embracing money raising, including the controversial step of charging an admission fee. This fee is not charged on Sunday or during services. In addition, a special appeal yielded four million pounds and an insurance windfall after a storm helped pay for repair of Ely's famous octagon tower. Nearby medieval buildings are being converted into restaurants, shops, and rent-yielding properties. Modern management techniques have been adopted, and cathedral organization is now divided in groups responsible for worship, music, education, finance, and marketing. According to the vice dean and treasurer, every new idea passes through the stages of concept, research, and implementation, and computers code activities so that results can be monitored on a monthly basis. In addition, the staff all have portable telephones so that decisions that can't wait for meetings can be made expeditiously.[19]

Among cathedrals, Durham is financially relatively well-off. This it owes in part to the fact that it managed to keep most of its estates when those of other cathedrals were seized by ecclesiastical commissioners in the nineteenth century. Combined, these estates provide an estimated 400,000 pounds in rent annually, with a similar amount coming from other investments. Admission to the cathedral is free. "Entry into the House of God should be an experience, not a transaction," according to the dean. But proceeds from a restaurant and book shop, combined with the collection box, provide about one third of the 1.3 million pounds needed annually to maintain the cathedral.[20]

Elsewhere, matters are less favorable. The Winchester dean voiced a common complaint in saying that he has to spend 80 percent of his time raising money, specifically, the 600,000 pounds needed annually to keep the cathedral open to visitors. A sign at the entrance suggests but does not require a donation of 1.50 pounds. The average donation, in fact, is 50 pence.[21] This is far better than at Rochester, Britain's oldest cathedral, where the average donation is just eight pence.

At St. Paul's, the chief executive was fired after his money-raising suggestions of expanding the gift shop and opening a restaurant met with the disapproval of dean and chapter. In Lincoln, a fund raising scheme which involved sending the cathedral's priceless copy of the Magna Carta to an exposition in Australia backfired, causing a scandal and instigating an inquiry that cost far more than the scheme generated.

At York, the dean and the chapter doubled the rents of local shops. And Salisbury's plans for a new visitor's center and restaurant have drawn the fire of its own bishop, who thinks peripheral activities already produce too much noise and distract from the spiritual mission. "Though a cathedral is a working building, its quality of life is not the same as a factory or supermarket." The Dean of Salisbury politely suggested that the bishop was talking about an ideal world, which bore little correspondence to the present reality.[22]

The government came to the British cathedrals' assistance in early 1991, but its partial solution presented new problems. The government made it known that it was willing to provide funding through the Department of the Environment and administered by English Heritage. With the estimate for the total repair of all cathedrals placed between 70 and 170 million pounds, Dr. Robert Runcie, Archbishop of Canterbury and head of the church of England, suggested a government contribution of 70 million pounds. The actual funding, when awarded in March of 1991, was 11.5 million pounds, a fraction of what was necessary. While expressing their gratitude, church leaders also voiced their fears of a loss of control now that an outside agency would be involved in decisions regarding the future of cathedrals.

Despite the fact of declining congregations, church authorities, their followers, and even large portions of the public still resist recognizing the extent to which the cathedrals' social role has changed from worship to tourism. Agreeing with the Dean of Rochester, such people feel it proper, or at least psychically reassuring, to view all tourists as potential pilgrims and the cathedral as a significant point in their quest for spiritual enlightenment.[23] In today's society, in which marketing appears to penetrate every activity, the cathedrals must stand physically and symbolically above it all. But to believe this is to deny the physical and financial problem and their social causes.

The Politics of Landmarking

The tension between the spiritual and the secular takes a different turn in the United States, where church leaders and preservationists have become entangled in a complicated politics surrounding the issue of landmarking.

Church properties can be either financial burdens or assets. In a New York City case dating back to 1980, a yeshiva housed in the historic Rice Mansion on Riverside Drive wanted to sell the mansion to a developer. This mansion was the last remaining example of what used to be a procession of stately houses. In its stead, the developer planned to erect a thirty-story apartment house. The local community argued against the sale, citing the house's historic and architectural significance. It also argued that the proposed height for the new building was inappropriate to the area. The yeshiva argued that preservation of one isolated house was historically pointless and out of context with the new neighborhood. Some yeshiva supporters argued in addition that putting a landmarks designation on the building, which would effectively stop the sale, was tantamount to a suppression of religious freedom and discrimination against the Jewish community.[24]

In the end, the mansion was declared a landmark and the sale was prevented. This was not an isolated case, for other churches and synagogues claimed that landmark designation was no honor, but rather increased financial hardship. In a January 1982 statement, the Committee of Religious Leaders of the City of New York called landmarking "a threat to religious freedom" and concluded, "We strongly object to the forced diversion by government of resources dedicated for religious ministry to serve instead the cause of architectural preservation." In brief, religion and preservation were seen as opposing causes engaged in battles both legal and symbolic.

These volleys were prelude to the battle of the decade, the

battle over St. Bartholomew's Episcopal Church in midtown
Manhattan. St. Bartholomew's is an elegant masonry structure
built in 1919 at 50th Street and Park Avenue. In 1981 the church
authorities proposed selling part of its adjacent property and air
rights to a developer. The architect, Peter Capone of the leading
firm of Edward Durrell Stone Associates, came up with a design for
a fifty-nine-story glass tower.

This proposal promptly met with opposition. Architectural
critics and preservationists argued that it would cut out necessary
light and space, and would block the attractive, architecturally
consonant office building recently completed nearby. Paul Goldberger, architectural critic of the *New York Times,* described the
proposed structure as "an intrusion of glittering glass into a group-
ing of buildings noted for their masonry quality; it will be belittling
not only to the church, but to the graceful and exuberant General
Electric Tower behind St. Bartholomew's." He concluded simply,
"This is the wrong building in the wrong place."[25]

The tower plans became bogged down, some said due to the
slowdown in the real estate market, others, to second thoughts on
the part of the developers. In the summer of 1984 the city's landmark commission denied approval to the plans, which sent the architect back to the drawing board. He reemerged with a new plan
radically different from the first. Capone cut the tower's height from
fifty-nine to forty-seven stories and exchanged glass for a limestone
and brick surface designed to complement the church's masonry.
A series of setbacks added to the impression of respect paid by the
new structure to the elegant old church.

While some in the congregation still opposed the tower on the
principle that any new construction took light, air, and attention
away from the church, church officials threatened to sue if the new
design were voted down.

Despite such threats, in June of l985 the Landmarks Preservation Commission rejected this second, more conservative proposal.
Panel members made it clear that they objected to both the design
and to any proposal that involved razing any part of the religious
landmark.

The case eventually went to the Supreme Court, which upheld

the ruling of the United States Court of Appeals for the Second Circuit in Manhattan. This court had ruled that the landmark designation violated neither the church's right to religious exercise nor to use of its own property. The church had argued that its First Amendment rights were abrogated by placing control of its activities in the hands of a secular agency with a different set of priorities. But, as one opponent of the plan summed up the significance of the decision, "The court confirmed a longstanding set of decisions that when spiritual organizations step into the secular world, they are bound by the same rules as everyone else."[26]

On the other side, one reaction to the decision was fear that, in elegant neighborhoods, the "preserve-at-any-cost mentality" would "turn landmark houses of worship into the equivalent of architectural bric-a-brac for the rich."[27] The sacred would be reduced to the most banal form of secular trappings. But Paul Goldberger saw a religious purpose in the landmark designation and rejoiced in the court's decision, writing, "It is not too flippant to say that in the preservation of St. Bartholomew's as an intact piece of cityscape there is some benefit to the soul not unlike that which the church aspires to within its doors."[28] Architecture, in short, can be redemptive.

The phraseology is important. This "some benefit to the soul" is a soft theology, a theology without dogma, constraint, or call for personal sacrifice. It reflects back on one of the outcomes of secularization mentioned at the beginning of this chapter, namely the depoliticization of religion. Religious authorities are decreasingly political powers, increasingly political supplicants. In this decision, the court held that the same rules applied to sacred as to secular bodies and organizations. The soft theology of "some benefit to the soul" also reflects the individualization of religion, its reduction to the level of personal sentiment. It is presumably up to each individual to decide whether or not St. Bartholomew's provides some spiritual or psychic benefit. That benefit, presumably, must be free for the asking—free, at least, for those able to appreciate fine architecture. In earlier times, religious pilgrims may not have had to pay admission charges, but they were supposed to undergo ordeals and make sacrifices on their journeys to holy sites. Today's pilgrims, however, are tourists, and less is to be expected.

Consuming ▦ *CHAPTER 7*
History

Press a button and chat with the beautiful
Claudia. She'll tell you that having a baby in
Roman Britain was no joke. . . .
Watch out when you step aboard the per-
fectly reconstructed old ferry deck. It could
leave you feeling queasy . . . and be pre-
pared for that old salt, Captain Crusty, to
hurry you along for the spectacular Time and
Tide Show.
　　　　—White Cliffs Experience brochure

History is no longer treated with respectful distance. Rather, it
is mined for images and ideas that can be associated with
commodities. Like the rest of culture, history is being bought and
sold. It is being remolded and reshaped to serve the fickle demands
of the market.

　　The commodification of history involves the confounding of
media images with historical realities. In localities large and small
"Heritage Machines" comprised of specific interest groups market
historic sites for combined profit. The commodification of history
is also evident in the process by which consumption itself is being
defined as a "trip into the past" through the creation of shopping
villages and urban malls set in rehabilitated historic buildings.
Underlying it all is a social psychology of the encounter between

past and present that is created through tourism and magically maintained through souvenirs and collections. Nostalgia may be an ill-
ness, as Freud believed. Or it may reflect that fact that consumerism
still carries with it the shadow of moral and spiritual longings
unmet and unsatisfied by modern society.

Media History and "Real" History

Viewing the mixtures of real and fake can result in a form of historical
vertigo. This is especially true when objects of media history are
preserved along with objects of real history. South of San Luis
Obispo, California, crews excavated the dunes where the silent
movie *The Ten Commandments* was filmed in 1923. The Cecil B.
De Mille site of an Egyptian city included over twenty sizable
sphinxes, four thirty-five-foot statues of pharaohs, and a huge bas-
relief wall extending more than 750 feet. Much of the set appears
to have been secretly buried on the site when filming was over. The
Smithsonian Institution and several other museums expressed an
interest in exhibiting some of the set's remains.[1]

The Smithsonian already displays media artifacts including
Mickey Mouse ears, a Howdy Doody doll, and Archie and Edith
Bunker's living room chairs. Media history is part of consumer
history and an important part of twentieth-century history. The display of such popular objects tells us that we, in our consumer
habits, have participated in something important. By turning on the
television or going to the movies, we have, in our own small way,
been making history.[2]

In the spring of 1992 one media exhibit boldly went where no
exhibit had gone before: With much fanfare, the National Air and
Space Museum mounted a *Star Trek* exhibit in its second-floor
gallery. Lines of eager tourists viewed Spock's ears, Captain Kirk's
chair, and a selection of costumes worn by crew and aliens. What
was most striking about the exhibit, however, was how few *physical* objects were actually exhibited. Instead, most of the walls were
covered with photographs, descriptions of the history of the show,
and presentations of some of its major themes. These themes
included sexuality, race, and power. They demonstrated how this

successful television serial reflected social concerns dominant in late sixties and seventies American society.

The relative lack of physical objects reinforces a point made earlier about the subtle difference between the media and museums. The physicality of the exhibited objects provides as least the potential of a direct link between contemporary viewer and historical period, above and apart from the interpretive surround. With the media, this direct physical link is missing. We have only the images of the screen or in the magazine.

What was also striking was how *Star Trek* was represented *outside* the particular gallery space as well as in it. Museum-goers lined up for in the first-floor lobby for special timed tickets. (This device for limiting flow is used by other cultural attractions, including the French caves remaining open to the public and the popular gardens at Sissinghurst Castle.) Tourists waiting for their exhibit viewing time were entertained by large screens placed on both exhibit floors which ran old *Star Trek* episodes. Each screen drew a constant crowd, with many children and teenagers sitting down in the middle of the museum floor as if at home. *Star Trek* episodes were more captivating and immediate to them than all the museum's assembled rocketry, space capsules, and experimental aircraft.

The mounting of the *Star Trek* exhibit at the National Air and Space Museum was, in fact, an extension of a program which had already mounted exhibits on how warfare in World War I and II was represented by Hollywood films. An exhibit on World War I flying aces showed how these men became media objects and objects of consumption. It included a display case of consumer items, including model airplanes and Snoopy in his flying ace gear. The wide range of *Star Trek* related consumer products only added to the extensive range already offered in the crowded gift shop. There was an additional marketing kiosk of *Star Trek* products near the front lobby, which was doing a land-office business.

How the arts have presented flight is part of the social history of aviation. The difficulty comes when the very accessible media presentations such as *Star Trek* threaten to overwhelm the actual history. The historical artifacts exhibited are more didactic in nature, and require more work, than the already familiar and comforting television images. Visitors got a chance to compare their knowledge about plots, rather than exposing their ignorance about aviation history and technology.[3] A popular, consumer-oriented exhibit like the *Star Trek* one may draw more people into the museum, who, paradoxically, may be less able to see and learn about the actual history of flight as they participate not in the romance of flight, but the romance of television.

Outside the museums, media history is sold in other ways. Holiday makers can rent the Victorian lodge that served as the home for Audrey Forbes-Hamilton in the British television series, *To the Manor Born.* They can visit Castle Howard and think they are revisiting Brideshead. After the series set at Castle Howard aired, tourist attendance at this Yorkshire country home rose 35 percent. Media and reality will be further confounded if the present owner of Castle Howard succeeds in his plans for a Brideshead Golf Course and Country Club designed to woo Japanese and American tourists. The plans include a two hundred-bed hotel and conference center. Preservationists are unenthusiastic about the project, which Simon Howard defends as a necessary means to the end of maintaining British heritage.[4]

At Castle Howard the media added name recognition to a site of historic and architectural importance. But the media can also make something special, even something sacred, out of the most ordinary localities. The popular movie *Field of Dreams* was about a young farmer who was instructed by a long-dead baseball player to construct a baseball field. Other dead baseball players would play ball, and people would presumably come to fill the stands: "If you build it, they will come." Following upon the movie's popularity, people did come—to the film location in a field in Dyersville, Iowa. In summer of 1990 tourists were driving up in numbers as high as a thousand a week.

Why they came is anyone's guess. Some tourists expressed a sense of awe more usually associated with religious monuments. To some extent, the field is a monument to the romance of baseball and men's dreams of success. It is also a monument to the great dream machine of Hollywood and its ability to turn the most banal site into something providing intimations of immortality. As one character in the film explains to the farmer, "People will come, Ray. They'll come to Iowa for reasons they cannot even fathom. They'll turn up your driveway, not knowing for sure why they are doing it. They'll arrive at your door, as innocent as children, longing for the past." Today, they line up with video-cameras, photograph each other hitting, catching, and running bases, and leave with souvenir tee shirts and caps.[5]

If an Iowa farm can be given mythic significance, then any site contains tourist potential. If there is an actual historic association, if *anything* unique, or simply interesting, happened, then maybe you don't even need Hollywood's help in realizing latent tourist potential. This fact is being realized by groups in both Britain and the United States, who are banding together and working to make a profit while promoting local history. These groups are the new "Heritage Machines," descendants of the prodevelopment "Growth Machines" of the 1970s.

Heritage Machines

In the seventies growth machines comprised of politicians, business-people, speculators and developers shaped urban land use and patterns of development.[6] Today, heritage machines are being constructed in cities and towns, large and small. Unlikely bedfellows, including academics, preservationists, developers, and politicians, profit from the exploitation—and sometimes the invention—of local heritage. In Britain, heritage machines are less likely than in the States to gain control due to the continued view of many preservationists that developers represent potential enemies rather than potential allies. In America, preservationists pray for the restoration of tax credits to once again attract developers into preservation projects. Even without generous tax credits, however, many Americans find preservation a profitable enterprise.

In some cases, the profit takes the form of traditional pork barrel politics. Author Brian Kelly argues that Steamtown National Historic Site in Scranton, Pennsylvania, owes its existence (if not original brainstorm) to the pork barrel tactics of the local congressman, Republican Joseph McDade. According to Kelly, McDade has been willing to trade his support of other congresspeople's projects for their support of Steamtown. This site passed through Congressional approval on an omnibus bill and carried an original price tag of $35 million. Actual expenses soon went much higher. The following year another $40 million was requested to finish Steamtown, and $6.5 million for annual maintenance.

The overextended National Park Service did not appreciate this forced and expensive addition to its collection of parks and landmarks. Furthermore, many experts were skeptical about the addition's merit. Among them was John White, a former transportation curator at the Smithsonian, who called Steamtown "a third-rate collection in a place to which it has no relevance."[7] History can be a pork barrel full of local jobs, tourist dollars, tax revenues, and recognition for the representative who manages to bring home the bacon.

Heritage machines may start small. The present always contains the potential for future exploitation: the little boy or girl in the house next door may grow up to be president, thus making the natal home subject for sanctification. Originally only the houses of the most distinguished presidents were selected for preservation: Washington, Jackson, Lincoln. Now every president has the right to a shrine, a homestead and/or library, no matter how illustrious or forgettable his tenure.

So too, apparently, do vice presidents. In the small town of Huntington, Indiana, enterprising individuals are already making the best of what they've got. What they've got is Dan Quayle. The "Premier Dan Quayle Memorabilia Exhibit" was mounted in 1991 in the town's public library. It included such items as Quayle's Little League uniform, baby hair, a piece of carpeting, a coffee cup, and numerous photographs and letters. Quayle boosters have organized themselves into the Dan Quayle Commemorative Foundation. Besides mounting the exhibit, the foundation offers walking tours past historic Quayle sites, including a family ranch house and a small restaurant he used to frequent.

The relatively small scale of the Quayle foundation efforts means that it has not yet run into substantial opposition from other interests. Even local Democrats are being discreetly polite about it. Elsewhere, the situation is more complicated. In 1989, the civic leaders of Deadwood, South Dakota, persuaded the state legislature to legalize gambling, with a percentage of the profits going to support the Deadwood Restoration Fund. However, leaders and legislators hedged their own bets by dictating a maximum bet of five dollars. This limit was meant to discourage organized crime from taking over and, in general, to keep things under control.

Within a few years, more than eighty gaming halls were in operation. The Deadwood/Lead Area of Commerce circulated an attractive brochure inviting would-be tourists to "Come Play in the Past," with the double entendre of "play" reinforced by pictures of outdoor sports interspersed with pictures of cards and poker chips. The tourist could either gambol or gamble. The small scale and historic Old West settings guaranteed that Deadwood was good clean family fun, in contrast to the modern glitz and implicit danger of high stake places like Las Vegas.

From 1989 through 1991 profits from gambling contributed $35 million to the restoration fund, and raised Deadwood tax revenues by 50 percent. The local heritage machine, pushing for the maximum $100 bet, included owners of the gaming halls and related businesses, such as hotels and motels, restaurants, and associated tourist attractions. Opponents included church leaders and other civic leaders worried about maintaining both decency and local control. They also included leaders of the Sioux tribe. Members of the local branch of the tribe, the Flandreau, ran their own casino, which earned enough to give every member a $3,000 annual dividend. Indian elders expressed similar concerns about loss of control and decency, in particular, about the effect of increased drinking on their communities.

Outside figures were lined up as either heritage machine supporters or detractors. The Sioux looked for support from Senator Bob Kerrey, to whom they gave an honorary Indian title. Paradoxically, Kevin Costner, who celebrated Sioux culture in his vastly popular movie *Dances with Wolves,* aligned with heritage machines interests. Costner headed an investment group that wanted to build a new $35 million hotel-casino in Deadwood. The group also planned to restore an old railroad which would bring tourists from

Rapid City to Deadwood. Investors insisted on the $100 maximum bet to fill the hotels and guarantee the investment.[8] Costner, however, withdrew the development plan and, in a public vote taken 14 September 1993, the proposal to raise the bet maximum was defeated.

In major urban areas heritage machines are subject to an even greater complexity of economic and social forces. In Tampa, Florida, the heritage machine has focused attention on the remaining structures of what had once been a highly distinctive community. Ybor City was the site of the Latin Quarter, where Cuban, Spanish, and Italian immigrants lived and worked in Tampa's cigar factories. Many of the workers were socialists or anarcho-syndicalists and exhibited a militant trade unionism. Their keen interest in current events, politics, and social thought was fed by the orators, called "lectors," who read aloud to other workers in the cigar factories.

A sizable percentage of the Cuban workers had been Afro-Cubans. Following the decline of the cigar industry in the post World War I years, Ybor City became more solidly African-American. Urban renewal in the 1960s wiped out much of the distinctive housing where the cigar workers had lived. What remained was the core commercial area, stranded among empty lots where renewal had stalled and cut off from the Tampa downtown by major expressways.

Still, the historic Latin structures and their proximity to downtown were tantalizing to potential heritage machine interests, including planners, preservationists, and developers. As Susan Greenbaum argues, a "politics of culture" emerged in which these planners and preservationists attempted to downplay the political radicalism of the cigar workers and the contributions of Afro-Cubans and African-Americans to the community. These interests also sought to restrict any role of the present African-American population in interpreting Ybor City history or in participating in the Ybor City Festival, first held in 1986.

Others, including preservationists, interested academics, and representatives of the African-American community, supported the effort to preserve Ybor City. However, they argued strongly against what they perceived as racist interpretations and presentations that would sanitize and supposedly protect the area from urban crime. One object of their anger was a proposal briefly mooted that called for surrounding the whole potential tourist area with a huge wall. This second group had less financial clout among its members than that held by the developers. But it could count on the support of the National Endowment for the Arts, which helped sponsor the Ybor City Festival. As a federal agency, the NEA repeatedly argued for more multiculturalism in general and more African-American representation and participation in particular.

In such controversies, preservation's political implications are clear to all concerned. In the States, there seems to be more shared awareness of these implications, engendered in part by the more participatory nature of grassroots preservation. In Britain, by contrast, the more centralized authority granted to organizations such as English Heritage and National Trust has meant that both organizations can adopt a more conservative stance. Both organizations serve what they perceive as the needs of the nation, rather than the need to represent or serve particular constituencies or to represent Britain's growing ethnic diversity.

In America, preservation has not simply served to represent diversity, but to celebrate it. The most famous example of this on the national level involved the restoration of Ellis Island, New York's historic immigration center.

Selling Ellis

With pamphlets and mailings that asked accusingly, "If You Don't Keep Their Names Alive . . . Who Will?" the State of Liberty–Ellis Island Foundation made Americans an offer that many could not—and did not—refuse. For $100 Americans could nominate the name of an immigrant ancestor to be engraved on a copper-plated American Immigrant Wall of Honor. For $200, two names could be engraved. Contributions of $1,000, $5,000, and $10,000 entitled names to special placement. If the ancestors came through a different port of entry, that was acceptable. If one could no longer remember the ancestor, one could enter one's own name. That was also acceptable. In this democracy, all qualified for the wall of honor, living and dead, immigrant and non.

Appropriately enough, the public figurehead for the campaign was automobile executive Lee Iacocca. Who better than the manufacturer of the American dream machine to speak with conviction about the American Dream? Recalling how his parents arrived as Italian immigrants, Iacocca wrote, "They arrived with little money, but a wealth of hopes and dreams. Like parents everywhere, they dreamed of a better life for their children. And because this was America, they were able to make their dream a reality."

The Statue of Liberty–Ellis Island Foundation was successful because it was able to wrap its campaign within the cherished American values of tolerance, freedom, and economic opportunity. The historic monument of Ellis Island was a symbol of the American mythology that attracted many to its shores and that continues to provide a sense of emotional sustenance and meaning to their descendants.

By the fall of 1989 over two hundred thousand names had been submitted, and registration for the wall was closed. In 1990, though, a second and similar appeal was launched along the same lines for a special centennial section of the wall.

While many Americans responded enthusiastically, critics asked whether the American Immigrant Wall of Honor truly stood for the values it proclaimed. It seemed highly inappropriate to some people that a monument with such a shared, public significance be funded by individual contributions receiving individual recognition in the form of names displayed. Were the immigrants not listed somehow dishonored by their exclusion? Were their families publicly shamed? Were African-Americans, Native-Americans, and Asian-Americans less likely to be listed, even if all were technically eligible, free immigrants, natives or slaves, East or West Coast arrivals?

Further, with ethnic strife mounting throughout the nation, and especially in New York City, the melting pot imagery of the wall seemed more a mockery of earlier dreams than their fulfillment. Instead of equality, the wall honored inequality: the ability of some to pay while others couldn't. None of this seemed quite right for a national monument meant to honor the ideal of democracy.

Since its reopening, the restoration has continued to draw crowds who wait patiently at the ferries to transport them from New York harbor to the island. But by March 1991 the famous Wall of Honor was being labeled a "Wall of Dishonor" by the press. Social reality had overtaken social mythology, as the names of immigrant ancestors were being defaced and covered with graffiti by vandals. With its customary dramatic flair, the New York Post called the wall "a pockmarked graffiti-strewn eyesore."9 One tourist likened the acts of vandalism to those routinely performed in cemeteries—a desecration of the memory of the dead. An Ellis Island spokeswoman dealt with the situation by explaining, "This is New York City and it happens." The wall was dismantled, treatments tested, and a stronger protective coating applied.

Desecration can take many forms. Destruction caused by vandals can be small stuff compared to that committed by those with economic and political clout. Ellis Island provides an excellent example of a conflict over the extent and proper use of a site with near-sacred significance in its nation's history.

The actual restoration of the Great Hall at Ellis Island received high marks from preservationists and architects. But the Hall was only the most significant room within the most significant building in a whole landscape of buildings. In late 1991 public attention focused on some of the other buildings. Should they be left to ruin, restored, or altered for adaptive reuse? Specifically, the National Park Service, responsible for the running of Ellis Island, supported a proposal to turn twelve buildings on the south side of the island into a conference center, including a hotel of 325 rooms. The enterprise, costing some $145 million, would be privately owned.

To build the conference center would require the destruction of the twelve historic immigration buildings, including the contagious disease wards, the laundry, furnace, morgue, and crematorium. The debate over the plan split preservationists down the middle. Those against it included many in the State Historical Office in Albany. Orin Lehman, Commissioner of Parks, Recreation, and Historic Preservation, argued that the proposal trampled on the "evocative nature of the island" and threatened an overcommer-cialization that would corral the ghosts of immigrants past in the Great Hall.[10] The then-president of the National Trust, J. Jackson Walter, questioned the private development of a site with such wide public significance. "Economics simply can't be what Ellis Island is all about."

On the other side of the debate, the National Park Service argued that economics was *very* relevant to the future of Ellis Island. Gerald Patten, the NPS regional director, said the NPS capital budget was only $200 million against a backlog of $2 billion needed for rehabilitation and repairs at landmarks and parks. No public money could be committed to Ellis Island, at least not through the NPS budget. The conference center promised to create new jobs, greater tax revenues, and increased tourism. Perhaps not surprisingly, leading local politicians backed the plan, including Congressman Charles B. Rangel of Manhattan and Frank Guarini of Jersey City.

In this case, the protests raised by preservationists were so strong that the National Park Service finally withdrew its support, effectively killing the proposal for a conference center and hotel. Ellis Island would remain, at least for some time, a monument to all the people, even if its Wall of Honor suggested that, in this great democracy, some were more equal than others.

Historic Shopping Villages and Urban Malls

Consumer culture and postmodernism form interweaving and interpenetrating social processes. Postmodernism views consumer culture as one of the defining aspects of contemporary society. But postmodernism itself feeds back into consumerism by producing distinctive postmodern goods in literature, the arts, and the media.[11]

One of the characteristics of postmodernism is a nostalgic longing for past forms of social organization. In Britain, once but no longer a nation of shopkeepers, nostalgia is evident in historic representations that replicate Victorian shops. On the South Coast, the resort town of Eastbourne has a "How We Lived Then" Museum of Shops with over fifty thousand exhibits. Tourists are invited to relate what they see to their own nostalgic experiences: "Can you still taste Tizer or Virol and remember the 'Ovaltineys' or 'Bisto Kids?'. . . Remember 'Five-boys' chocolate and when sweets were weighed from jars?" Not far inland from Eastbourne, Buckleys of Battle invites visitors to "Return to the Corner Shop," be it the chemist's, the sweet shop, the pub or the pawnbroker's. Such historic representations re-create the small-scale intimacy of the village shops of days past, even as increasing numbers of out-of-town shopping centers are undermining the economic viability of actual village shops.

In the States, historic shopping experiences take different forms. Nostalgic shops rarely stand isolated on their own as historic representations: rather they are more frequently either part and parcel of Staged Symbolic Communities, or old and new are integrated in what are called "shopping villages" (since most real villages have been destroyed) and in urban malls created in the shells of historic structures.

In the post World War II years, the trend was for shopping to move away from villages and town main streets out toward new suburban shopping centers. These new shopping centers offered easy access, easy parking, wide item choice, and an environment that was clean, safe, and modern. The process spelled doom for the unfashionable main streets. What had once been centers of civic pride frequently became centers of dereliction.

Meanwhile, shopping centers evolved into shopping malls. They became bigger and grander, competing with each other for how many stores they could contain under a covered roof, how many major department stores anchored the projecting wings, and how many acres of parking surrounded these fortresslike constructions.

The growing need for mall security dimmed part of the original appeal, suburban safety from urban crime. Mall police and security guards became more evident, shop security systems universal, and customers began to worry about having their cars broken into or being mugged in those dark wastelands of parking lots.

Malls countered the inevitable loss of modern glamour by becoming not just bigger but more exotic. Food halls with colorful flags, banners, and mobiles offered shoppers the fast food of all nations. Atriums, with their hanging cascades of greenery and gurgling fountains, created the image of an oasis. This attracted clusters of senior citizens, who camped out on the benches without buying much. The only ones who seemed to really enter into the mall spirit were the packs of teenagers and preteenagers, who made the mall their hangout.

Unknown to the teenage hordes, some architects were trying to revive Main Street. The National Trust for Historic Preservation Main Streets Project was first launched in 1977, and in 1980 the National Main Street Center was created. Since then, it has overseen the restoration and redevelopment of Main Streets in almost eight hundred communities in thirty-four states. Through its efforts, more than $2.5 billion has been reinvested in physical improvements, more than seventeen thousand new businesses were created, and with them a net gain of more than sixty thousand new jobs.[12]

The Main Streets program had all the difficulties inherent in preservation projects: local conflicts of interest and simply different ideas as to what constituted a desirable streetscape. There were the inevitable limits of time, will, energy, and dollars. There was also no guarantee that the restoration would payoff—that suburbanites would flock back to the Main Streets once the cracked cement was dug up and replaced with bricks, and once power lines were buried and fake gas lamps installed.

Some developers preferred to work in less piecemeal and voluntaristic a fashion. The refusal of one recalcitrant shopkeeper could ruin the whole visual effect and also cut into profits. Developers took to the grander ideas of postmodern architects, who proposed revolutionizing consumption by returning it to its human scale. Don't revive Main Street, they advised. Make the mall over *into* Main Street.

The model for the make over was the transformation of the New Seabury Shopping Center on Cape Cod into Mashpee Commons. Developers bought the old shopping center and hired an architectural team. The architects had the asphalt torn up and divided up the larger store, creating more of a village shop effect. They added streets, sidewalks, plazas, and benches. Small storefronts now had inviting shop windows. There was a lot of postmodern architectural detail that recalled the old New England village.

To the visitor in the summer of 1991, it still looked like a shopping mall in the center of a vast parking lot. But there was a new concept behind it that was attracting developers, corporate retailers, architects, and planners from as far as Japan. As one of the developers said, "To the retail world we're a mid-size shopping center. . . . But we call this a downtown."[13]

The whole design was seen not simply as boosting retail sales, but as promoting a return to social connectedness and neighborliness. It would be especially valuable for the old, for whom the local housing authority had already by 1991 built twenty-four apartments close to the center. It would also be good for the young. It would keep them out of malls (even if it once had been a mall). As the developer argued, "We don't want to see (children) going to the suburban mall and living within the four walls of a car." He continued, obviously warming to the topic, "I think it's the responsibility of everyone to open the front door, get out in the yard, take a walk down the street, and get involved."[14]

Such voluntarism based on an individual sense of responsibility and civic pride would, however, be accompanied by tight planning controls and architectural guidelines. One thing that hadn't changed in the movement from modernism to postmodernism was the desire of architects to assign themselves a considerable measure of social control. However, while architecture may suggest social patterns, people do not always follow the suggestions, as the experience of Seaside, Florida, made clear. While building codes tried to enforce a small-town atmosphere, with porches for sitting and narrow streets for walking, people retreated to back porches for privacy or indoors to watch television. There's more, in short, to turning back time, to creating a supposedly organic village, than building a clock tower or a postmodern post office. Beyond providing architectural guidelines and encouraging strolling, the problem is one of reactivating the sense of social responsibility that the rise of consumer society itself has helped stifle. It is one thing to "retrofit" a market, another thing to retrofit a mentality.

Transforming shopping malls into historic representations of villages is a trend still new enough to carry risks for developers. And megamalls are a countertrend now in both Britain and the United

States. Malls still have certain advantages. They are known commodities and are constructed to set formulas. As one developer involved said, "Because there's no formula for doing a downtown, they're much more difficult." He added, "It's easier to sign Pizza Hut to a deal than Joe's Pizza."[15]

With such social trends and fashions, that which first seems risky later becomes formulaic, even prosaic. When developer J. Rowse first proposed an urban equivalent of retro suburban shopping villages, he failed to receive financial backing. Today, his Quincy Market in Boston is an exemplar for other historical representations of urban markets in historic factories, warehouses, and civic buildings that have been adapted to the uses of consumer society.

At New York's South Street Seaport, museum and marketplace are totally confounded. Those looking for a taste of history will find it in a range of indoor galleries and outdoor maritime exhibits. The work of serious tourism is more than balanced by the play afforded by a wide range of restaurants, boutiques, and markets. On a summer's day, the Seaport area appears one giant playground. Japanese tourists wait patiently to have their picture taken with a young woman covered head-to-toe with green paint, in a Statue of Liberty costume. Others watch a street performer imitate a music box doll.

The South Street Seaport and similar sites combine the nostalgic leisure experience—boat or trolley rides—with myriad other forms of historic entertainments. The zone of mediation found in many Staged Symbolic Communities has been eliminated, with history and consumption totally intermingled. Such representations are better than most malls, because they are also sites. Tourists see and are seen in these new urban agoras, whose original business, be it fishmongering, canning, or producing chocolates, seems, for the most part, to have moved elsewhere.

The extent to which such historic representations, once risky business, have now become formulaic is pointed up in the comment of an NEA official monitoring the preservation and presentation of Ybor City. He feared that this distinctive site would soon join the "generic mini-malls in old structures with various chains and tourist trinket emporiums alongside living history presentations."[16]

In Britain, civic leaders and businesspeople want to work the same magic at historic docklands and abandoned factories in London, Gloucester, and Bristol, and also in many northern cities where the loss of industrial might has left a plethora of empty factory buildings. It has also, however, left an economically depressed population unable to shop at the trendy boutiques that often fill these representations.

Such markets are successful because they are fun. They intertwine tourism with consumerism. They satisfy the "libido for looking" and the desire to spend. Despite their atriums and fountains, malls represent by contrast the rational organization of consumption. They centralize purchases, pulling in shoppers from a wide area by means of major access roads and expressways. They standardize purchases, as shoppers are assured of finding basic goods within a predictable range.

Herbert Marcuse predicted an end to scarcity. This, he believed, would liberate people, enabling them to transcend past struggles and assume new dimensions of being. At the end of the twentieth century, this has not happened. More people are lacking the basics of life, food and shelter, and more British and Americans find themselves economically pressed, rather than economically liberated.

What *has* changed over the past century is the sheer volume and range of goods available. In today's marketplace, new goods and brands compete to find, as one student of advertising said, "a place to live in your mind." Many goods promise not just to fill a need or perform a service. They offer a form of magic, a promise, even of transcendence. While the major subject of this chapter is the historic structures that contain the goods, it is worth considering in what way historic goods—whether retro fashions and reproductions, souvenirs, or antiques and collectibles—offer this magic, promise this transcendence.

The Aura of the Historical Object

Certain categories of goods with historical associations are frequently invested with meaning or blessed with an aura far beyond their superficial qualities or social purposes. This aura is not intrinsic to the object, but extrinsic, located in the relationships people form with goods that they, individually and collectively, consider special.[17] Examples of such goods include retro-style products, souvenirs, antiques, and collections.

Retro-style products. Literary critic Susan Sontag has argued that all style contains elements of perversity. Style is an assertion of the self, a form of saying "no" to the ordinary. Retro fashions say "no" to the commonplace. They represent either status striving or social criticism.

When the historical style is associated with tradition, it is frequently associated with up-market taste. One of the fastest growing magazines in the 1980s was *Country Living,* which taught the aspiring young upper-middle classes how to live the good life, if not in the country, then "as if" in the country. One advertisement for the magazine showed horseback riding accessories strewn across an antique bench, beneath hunting lithographs. The copy read, "The Brennans have worked very hard to make it look like they never had to." It associated *Country Living* magazine with couples who "choose to celebrate their success by living in the style that discriminating Americans have always preferred." That style draws on "our rich Colonial legacy." *Country Living* promised to guide readers "in making that heritage part of their lives." The tag line added to the key words already mentioned—words like "success," "legacy," "heritage"—by inviting readers to "Come into Your Inheritance." This is precisely what numbers of young and no-longer-young people were hoping to do. *Country Living* would tell them how to spend their inheritance once they finally got it.

Among the most successful merchandisers of traditional-style goods is Ralph Lauren. Lauren's popularity is due to a widespread romanticization of history as a time of gentility, romance, and innocent sporting fun. That romantic appeal can be extended to men and women and children, and to a wide range of goods. Part of Lauren's style is tradition exaggerated into mannerism, history taken to extremes, postmodernism applied to fashion and to personal identity.

While older generations engage in the perversity of luxury through exaggerated imitations of traditional privilege, younger generations choose their retro styles designed more to *épater les parents* rather than the *bourgeoisie*. Parents who think of themselves as still young are shocked to see offspring in bell-bottoms and to find out that the 1970s have been rediscovered.[18]

Souvenirs. Other people's souvenirs can be social embarrassments: "Whatever possessed them to buy that?" People *are* possessed when they buy souvenirs. They are possessed by an experience that is transcendent insofar as it represents, at the very least, a break in the everyday. It may be simply the liberating release from work offered by historic entertainments, a trip back in time and lots of fun. It may also represent a vision of another way of living, another way of being.

Tourists want this liminal state to continue, but know it can not. This special state can only be recalled through memory. The souvenir provides the visual hook for remembrance of times past, both historically and experientially. The souvenir also provides a sign of status, a social indicator that you can afford trips to Colonial Williamsburg or Cornwall. It may be a personal reminder or a personal promise made to return someday, or to try to recreate the past in the present.

At their point of purchase, souvenirs are surrounded by a comforting cocoon of innocence. They pretend to be a natural product of the setting. They tell a story, if not of Sturbridge per se, then of early America, when objects had integrity and were homemade. It is a disappointment to find the souvenir is made in Singapore. That can affect the purity of the relationship between object and owner. The souvenir becomes just another bit of tourist tat.

Antiques. Antiques promise to avoid this betrayal of trust. An antique, even if originally mass-produced, is no longer a mass-market item. It has acquired individuality through history and through scarcity. Rather than being tragedy, as Freud argued family history is for the individual, history for antiques is a form of triumph. They are the few objects of their class to have survived time. These survivors are by definition superior. They possess silent secrets that we hope to share by giving them a home, by allowing them to live again through new social contexts and new social relationships. In this setting, they may speak to us.

A cynic once said, "Some are born with antiques, some acquire antiques, and some have antiques thrust upon them." There is a difference between antiques that are passed down through the family and those that are purchased. This difference involves knowledge and choice. One is likely to know more about the family antique than the one purchased in the antique shop "This table was made by my grandfather in the early 1900s; the chairs were an anniversary present to both grandparents about the same time. My mother always said I would inherit them." Compare this to "The dry sink we bought in Mattituck because we liked the look of it. The dealer said it came from a Maine farm house." But who really knows? Family antiques are likely to have more specific, if incomplete, narratives attached to them. With purchased antiques, we make up the narratives.

With store-bought antiques, we have less knowledge but more choice. All the goods in urban and rural antique shops are available to us, if we can but pay. There's less choice with family objects. Some are thrust upon us—Aunt Frieda's prized neo-rococo lamp with the wooing lovers, Uncle George's stuffed pheasant under glass. Our relationship with these historic objects differs from that of Frieda or George, who detected the aura in the lovers' lamp and the stuffed pheasant.

Some people are indeed born with antiques. Previous generations were often all too ready to get rid of the antiques they were born with. This was especially true in the postwar years—the Fablon Fifties in Britain, when this adhesive plastic was used to cover everything, and in America, where devalued "heavy old" furniture was replaced by Swedish Modern. Later generations rue the day their parents ditched the brass beds stored ignominiously in the garage. With antiques, as with ethnic affiliation, there often seems to be a skip in generations. This is essential for the cognitive jump from "junk" to "retro" or even "antique." Evidence for this phenomenon is found in the fact that Swedish Modern is on its way back.

Whether we buy antiques or treasure family antiques, the fact that we *have* antiques is meant to confer social status. At best, we should not simply possess antiques, but also possess knowledge about antiques. We should be able to see what others don't see, to detect the true patina of history, the cabinetmaker's stylistic signature. This knowledge is a form of power and, in the right circles, confers prestige.

Collections. If antiques inspire love, collections become obsessions. Those seriously involved in collecting often describe themselves as obsessed, or even ill. But to the collector, the obsession has its own magnificence, whether it is comprised of Louis XIV furniture or refrigerator magnets. The collection glorifies the self and provides an escape from the self.

Much as antique owners acquire prestige through their antiques, serious collectors gain prestige through their choice of obsessive object, though many deny the fact of choice: Lightning struck, and they had to have the object of their desire. While satisfying their own taste, collectors are also playing to particular taste cultures, which will judge them and their collections.

The collector thus perfects a social self, as the collection becomes both prop and stage. But the collector also escapes the self through immersion in the collection. Most of us are born to one period and time and live our lives with others locked in a forward march. Collectors of historical objects reject the march of progress by recalling another period of their own choosing. The apartment of one New York decorator and dealer is totally devoted to a perfect collection of 1930s furniture and accessories. There is not a wrong note, no visible television or microwave. For London's New Georgians, the perfect time is the eighteenth century. Their historic collections and decorations represent a form of control over the immediate environment, a control rarely available in the outside world.

The perfect collection offers a form of escape more felt in its sum than its parts. Spirituality is associated with the idea of totality: There is clarity, completeness, and order. The perfect collection appears unsullied by time, restored to its pristine state. Collectors describe themselves as perfectionists. Surely their zeal is not limited to the mere accumulation of material goods and social status, but reflects as well these more inchoate, vaguely spiritual, longings and responses not met in the messy world of the now.

Thus historical objects serve such everyday purposes as status competition, role playing, and identity formation. But they can also, and at the same time, hint at something beyond. Whether that something is goodness, beauty, or truth, or even something "quite ineffable," it is not intrinsic to the object. Rather, it is wrapped up with the special relationship people form with the objects that they perceive as special, as having aura.

We Are the World █ CHAPTER 8

*Properties nominated to the World Heritage
list, 1992:
Butrinti, Albania; Algiers Kasbah, Algeria;
Angkor, Cambodia; historic cores of Prague,
Cesky Krumlov, and Telc, Czechoslovakia;
Cathedral of St. Stephen, Bourges, France;
Rammelsberg Ore Mine and the historic town
center of Goslar, Germany; Pythagoreion and
Heraion of Samos, Greece; pre-Hispanic city
of El Tajin, Mexico; Rio Abiseo National Park,
Peru; the old town of Zamosc, Poland; the
historic monuments of Novgorod and its
environs, the Solovetskii historical, cultural,
and natural complex, and the white monuments of Vladimir and Suzdal, Russian Feder-
ation; the archaeological site of Ban Chiang,
Thailand, and the Taos pueblo, United States
of America.*
                    —ICOMOS News 3:1 (March 1993)

So far discussion has focused on historic preservation in Great
Britain and the United States. But historic preservation and less
authentic historic representations are assuming truly global dimensions. On the one hand, historic preservation is becoming increasingly globalized through international conventions, meetings and
conferences, and training programs and exchanges. On the other
hand, preservationists prefer to emphasize the local quality of
much preservation and the national differences that remain. Both

trends reflect tensions within this emergent global professional culture as it works out contradictions within its own ideology and in its relationship with national political cultures.

All these developments within the preservation profession are occurring against the broader backdrop of less authentic historical representations. In Japan, businesses will soon be sending their employees to learn English in a mock Tudor village, complete with manor house, pub, and bowling green. In Verona, Italy, tourists beat a track to "Juliet's villa," which was identified as such on a quite arbitrary basis in the late nineteenth century. A balcony—so essential to Shakespeare's *Romeo and Juliet*—was added in the 1920s. And in the former East Germany, one entrepreneur is seriously contemplating a theme park dedicated to the overthrown Communist regime, complete with government spies and economic shortages.

To some the world is becoming one great theme park, with authentic cultural experiences being swamped by their replications and by the tourist tide they attract. Even as relatively inauthentic sites compete to attract the tourist dollar, authentic sites must find new techniques to guard against "tourist wear." That emblem of authenticity, Mount Vernon, conceals a steel frame to help the structure bear up under the traffic, and so many bits have been replaced, it's hard to know what floorboards, if any, might have known Washington's tread.

▨ *Global Conventions and Organizations*

The United Nations, operating through UNESCO, has adopted several conventions designed to protect cultural monuments worldwide. The best known of these is the Convention Concerning the Protection of the World Cultural and Natural Heritage, which was adopted by the UNESCO General Conference in 1972. This convention established a system of international cooperation and financed assistance for cultural and natural properties of outstanding universal value. As of fall 1993, there were 379 sites on the list of World Heritage Sites. American sites included the Mesa Verde National Park, Independence Hall, and the Statue of Liberty, among others. British sites considered of worldwide importance included Durham Castle and Cathedral, Ironbridge, Blenheim Palace, and Hadrian's Wall.

A second convention is somewhat less well known. The Convention on the Means of Protecting and Preventing the Illicit Import, Export, and Transfer of Ownership of Cultural Property was adopted by UNESCO in 1970. As the title suggests, this convention protects items of cultural heritage and/or archaeological importance against illegal exportation through one means or another.

The breakup of Yugoslavia focused attention on a third convention, namely the Convention for the Protection of Cultural Property in the Event of Armed Conflict. This is also referred to as the Hague Convention. Adopted in 1954, it was designed to protect cultural property, with all parties signing the convention agreeing to respect monuments in times of war and to protect them in peace. The lack of enforcement power behind such conventions was sadly demonstrated in the massive shelling of the ancient towns of Dubrovnik and Split. There were even reports that Serbs were using the Hague Convention flags flying from protected monuments as targets.[1]

These conventions provide recognition, some financial assistance, and some, albeit limited, protection. More significant in terms of sustained impact are the activities of several preservation organizations that have international representation and/or agendas.

Chief among these is the International Council on Monuments and Sites (ICOMOS). Founded in 1965, ICOMOS now comprises over sixty-eight national committees in a worldwide alliance. Its stated objectives include bringing together preservation specialists from around the world; serving as a clearinghouse for information on preservation techniques, principles, and policies; cooperating with national and international authorities to set up centers for preservation documentation; working for the adoption and implementation of the international conventions; and making professional expertise available worldwide.

In 1992, some of ICOMOS's international projects included conducting a survey in thirty-eight nations in the Pacific Asian region to determine the level of government support for the preservation of historic monuments and sites and beginning preparations to administer a project designed to preserve three fifteenth- to nineteenth-century forts in the central region of Ghana. Restoration of the Arneri Palace in Korcula, Croatia, was slowed by the civil war.

Along with these and other actual projects, ICOMOS also sponsored a plethora of international symposia and seminars, committee meetings, training conferences, summer intern programs, award programs, and publications in 1992. The American committee, US/ICOMOS, supported interns from Lithuania, Russia, Mexico, and the United Kingdom on work programs requested by the National Park Service. Young preservation professionals from the United States spent summer internships with preservation agencies in Poland, Lithuania, Israel, and France. Sixteen other young professionals from Argentina, Austria, Bulgaria, Canada, China, Croatia, Denmark, Finland, Guatemala, Hungary, Italy, Japan, Mexico, Russia, and Syria participated in summer documentation programs throughout the United States.

Such exchanges are a powerful mechanism for increasing both professionalization and globalization. As everything from preservation techniques to tourist management policies is taught in courses and shared worldwide, a global professional culture is emerging. This global professional culture is dedicated to preserving the *heterogeneity* of the built environment even as it employs an increasingly *homogenous* arsenal of approved techniques and approaches.

Other organizations directly involved in international preservation issues and efforts include UNESCO's Physical Heritage Divisions and its World Heritage Center, the World Bank Environmental Office, and the International Center for the Study of the Preservation and Restoration of Cultural Property (ICCROM), located in Rome. The World Monuments Fund, based in New York, is a private nonprofit organization. It is smaller, less bureaucratic, and more flexible than the mightier ICOMOS. Founded in 1965, the WMF pulls together funds from a variety of sources—governmental, corporate and philanthropic. By 1992 it had completed over twenty restoration projects and begun work on another forty around the world.[2]

Still other organizations have more of a specialty focus. The

Jewish Heritage Council is dedicated to documenting and restoring the monuments of Jewish people around the world. DOCOMOMO, short for Documentation and Conservation of Buildings, Sites, and Neighborhoods of the Modern Movement, is, as the name suggests, dedicated to preserving modernist structures. Other organizations are specifically interested in churches, country homes, and other types of structures.

As members of this emerging global professional culture, preservationists share values and belong to institutions that transcend national boundaries. As such, they may and frequently do find themselves at odds with the preservation practices and policies (or lack thereof) in specific nation-states.[3] Lowenthal provides a listing of the problems preservationists face with various national policies. Thus:

> In Italy listing is perfunctory, heritage is everywhere, yet legally nowhere. French designation ensures that buildings listed are reliably protected, but the categories under which listing is allowed are rigidly restrictive. In Spain historic structures named by Madrid are cared for (or neglected) entirely by 16 autonomous regions. New Zealand shuns listing because designators can be sued by property owners for asset loss. German listed buildings get so much state aid that some conservators fear overrestoration, except in eastern Germany, where they do not get enough.
>
> British listing is comprehensive but ineffectual.[4]

And so it goes. Preservationists battle national policies and fight destruction whether caused by war or economic pressures. ICOMOS continually finds itself in the position of voting for resolution and "expressing concern" about negative developments worldwide.

For example, in June 1990 ICOMOS expressed its concern to Egyptian authorities regarding construction work occurring within the pyramid fields from Giza to Dashur. The same year, ICOMOS expressed its concern to the Portuguese government regarding a building project located within the protected area surrounding the Monastery of the Hieronymites and the Tower of Belem. The subcommittee monitoring national sites "expressed concern" about the heavy poaching threatening the integrity of the Manovo–Gounda

St. Floris National Park in the Central African Republic, the Guinean government's intention to mine ore at the Mount Nimba Strict Nature Reserve, and the proposed construction of a highway crossing the Kahuzi–Bieg National Park in Zaire. Great concern was also expressed about the shelling of Dubrovnik and Split, but, as has already been suggested, to little avail.

Preservation can help increase national pride through creating a heightened awareness of national heritage. But historic sites can also serve as markers for local and/or regional identities. In many societies, these identities are still perceived as a threat to precariously constructed national identities. Evidence for this comes from the breakup not just of Yugoslavia but of the Soviet Union and from ethnic and regional tensions throughout the Third World.

Whether or not it helps build nationalist sentiment, preservation can add to the national exchequer through encouraging heritage tourism. While economic developments may threaten preservation of monuments by mining, road and project construction, preservation can aid economic development of a specific form. Social scientists debate the advisability of nations building economies based on tourism, but venture capitalists and entrepreneurs recognize that heritage can be profitable.

To international capital, cultural diversity is not a threat but a promise ripe with possibilities. Preservationists help realize this promise by making the world accessible for heritage tourism. Preservationists repair, reconstruct, certify, and interpret sites. International capital provides the facilities, the airline flights and ground transport, the hotels, shops and restaurants that make the whole process of foreign encounters less threatening and more pleasurable.

Cultural critic Stuart Hall suggests that it is in the very nature of capital, with its needs to expand, internationalize, and penetrate, to work through and utilize cultural differences. Capital celebrates and exaggerates cultural diversity, because cultural diversity creates a form of product differentiation, and product differentiation is a basic principle of marketing. Heritage sites encourage visitors to sample and to consume different cultures. But it is the local cultures themselves that end up paying the price.

▓ Heritage Tourism and the Disneyification of the World

Tourism is big business. It employs more people worldwide than any other industry. Tourism's infrastructure of transportation, lodging, and restaurants was valued at $3 trillion in 1989, with another $360 billion being invested in new structures and capital equipment during the same year. One out of every fifteen workers worldwide is employed in some aspect of tourism. A growth rate of 8.7 percent was expected to continue at least through 1992, despite the recession still affecting many industrialized Western nations.[5]

It is hard to separate out figures for heritage tourism, since visits to historic sites may be included with other stops on an itinerary, may form the basis of a tour, or may not be included at all. But those involved in the business tell us that it is booming, with excellent future prospects. Heritage tourists tend to be older and more affluent than regular tourists and tend to take several trips a year.

If heritage tourism is a golden goose, some are concerned as to whether it can—or should—be encouraged to continue laying golden eggs. One objection relates to the sheer physical overload of tourists on historic sites. At popular historic houses and gardens in Britain, tourists must now queue for timed tickets. The stampede of tourists has worn down the steps of Canterbury Cathedral and the Tower of London. Stratford-upon-Avon has become a virtual Shakespearean theme park, with new parking garages, pedestrianized ways, and shops catering to about 2.5 million visitors annually to this small Cotswold town.[6] The picturesque village of Clovelly, in Devon, now charges tourists admission to enter.

The sheer production of human heat and humidity is threatening the frescoes of the Sistine Chapel and the paintings in galleries throughout Italy. Venice is sinking and stinking with pollution. In Florence, tourists, some 1.5 million of them in 1991, wait in three separate and lengthy queues in order to see Michelangelo's *David.*[7] And in Paris, fumes from tour buses are damaging the stonework of Notre Dame Cathedral, which is being worn down by some 10.8 million visitors each year.[8]

Tourism used to be considered a great liberalizing force, enabling people both to appreciate cultural diversity and to see beyond cultural differences. This is no longer so accepted a view. Instead, the Archbishop of Canterbury has declared that tourism can raise the level of prejudice, cause pollution, encourage prostitution and economic exploitation, and lead to a "wholesale disregard for indigenous lifestyles." The Greek Orthodox Church now offers a new prayer: "Lord Jesus, have mercy on the cities, the islands and the villages of this Orthodox Fatherland . . . scourged by the worldly touristic wave."[9]

A second problem associated with heritage tourism is the potential "Disneyification" of the world. As more and more sites are taken over to develop their tourist potential, the world is being turned into one massive theme park. Disneyland in southern California and its younger Floridian sibling Disney World have a tremendous popularity. Since its founding in 1956, over 310 million visitors have passed through Disneyland, and over 300 million have seen Disney World. Walt Disney's mythic and fragmented vision of American history and culture has been exported to Japan, where close to 100 million people have toured Disney-Nippon.[10]

But when Disney began constructing a new Disney Monde theme park outside Paris, one of the citadel cities of Western culture, the juxtaposition of the fake and the real was almost too much to bear—certainly too much for one French critic, who labeled Disney Monde a "cultural Chernobyl." A Sleeping Beauty's castle, modeled after the image from the *Très riches heures du Duc de Berry,* was erected all shiny and new in a land of crumbling castle ruins. There are other tips of the hat to European culture, including an English village with market cross, half-timbered cottage with plastic thatch, and a pub serving warm beer.[11]

But most of the attractions present images of American culture and history refracted through a silvery cloud of pixie dust. These attractions include a Wild West Main Street, a mock-up of the Rockefeller Center skating rink, a turn-of-the-century Florida resort, a Sante Fe pueblo, and an East Coast yacht club. To one cultural critic, all this stuff signifies "a permanent shift in the cultural climate toward homogenization and the slicing of history into bite-size chunks easily digestible by the video generation."[12]

The 1993 attendance figures for Disney Monde were disastrous, and by the end of the year there was even talk of closure. But by this time Disney had announced plans for yet another theme park back in the USA. According to Disney spokesmen, the new theme park was to be located near the historic Civil War battlefield of Manassas, Virginia, and would depict American history as it really was, without any sugar coating. Disney's America would include a recreated Indian village, a nineteenth-century town, Civil War ironclad battleships, slaves, and a unique view of industrialization provided by a roller coaster ride through a mock factory with huge vats of molten steel.

While financial analysts applauded the proposal, editorial writers derided it. To many, the whole idea of a Disney theme park attempting to present an authentic interpretation of history was ludicrous. All previous Disney enterprises had led the Disney name to become synonymous with soft-focus, reassuring entertainment, rather than the factually more tragic American history. The physical juxtaposition of Disney America with the sacred battlefield of Manassas added a particularly ironic twist.[13] Under the concerted opposition of historians and preservationists, Disney finally withdrew the proposal, vowing, for the time being, to look for another, less controversial site.

Indeed, to many interested in historic preservation, Disney's constructions represent the negative reference point for their own historic representations. Commenting on the Austrian government's plans to have Schoenbrunn Palace managed by commercial operators, Karl von Hapsburg, grandson of the last Austrian emperor, commented, "I do not want them to turn it into a Disney or Hapsburg World with people running around with wigs."[14] Singapore is in the process of restoring the old warehouses and shops that make up its Clarke Quay, with the view of transforming this run-down precinct into a downtown entertainment district. While preservationists wanted to save the buildings, they did not want to restore the buildings' original bright colors. They argued instead for a more muted palette, "to prevent the district from looking like Disney."[15]

People in the past often favored a brighter coloration than present taste allows. It distresses up-market heritage tourists when the past does not mirror their expectations of faded gentility or pure classical monumentality. It requires considerable reprogramming to accept that both Greek temples and English cathedrals were once brightly ornamented with color instead of presenting stark stone facades. When research revealed that the rotunda of California's Old Capitol building had originally been brightly painted, preservationists assumed the dual tasks of repainting the room and reeducating the public. A similar process has been necessary at Williamsburg, where, as it turned out, the colonists had ideas of color that sometimes differed markedly from the colonial shades sold by paint companies.

Whether in Disney Technicolor or discreetly muted, the world is increasingly being redecorated for tourist visitors. Preservationists have begun to worry about their role in this process and about what it means to preserve monuments when the culture they were monuments *to* and *of* is destroyed. Sometimes this destruction precedes preservation; sometimes it is aided and abetted by it. Along with political upheavals, as in the former Soviet Union, economic transformations are occurring around the globe, with the flow of international capital penetrating into traditional patterns of social existence.[16] This process raises serious questions as to what it means, and what it costs, to preserve a village, town, or region.

In Japan, for example, the economic machine feeds on the "tear down and rebuild" mentality, a mentality that makes sense given the high land values.[17] Even sacred Kyoto is subject to development pressures on its historic and natural beauty. These pressures have intensified as the price of residential real estate has increased in the past three years. In particular, proposals to expand the main train station and remodel the Kyoto Hotel would make both into high rises. These proposals are being fought by Buddhist priests, who have developed a range of tactics. Many of these tactics are aimed at attracting the attention of tourists, who annually number approximately forty million and who contribute one quarter of Kyoto's income. The priests have locked tourists out of their historic temples, demanded they sign petitions protesting the developments, themselves posted billboards, and even taken out a full-page advertisement in the *New York Times*.[18] The advertisement accused Japanese enterprises of being only interested in realizing higher profits on their land investment, and the municipal government of serving only the interests of the businessmen.[19]

The deleterious impact of large modern hotels on landscapes and social economies in Third World societies has been decried. But even the "quality tourism" that appreciates local heritage and tries to build on it rather than destroy it can have a dubious effect. Preservationist William R. Chapman argues that the tourist industry in the Caribbean is creating a new Caribbean-style architecture bearing only superficial similarity to actual indigenous styles. As Chapman writes, "The true wealth of the islands . . . is in the 'particulars.' Each island has its own particular placement of porches and verandas, in the design of windows and staircases, and in the orientation and decoration of buildings." The Caribbean-style tends toward the generic and the gingerbread and has been fueled by the neotraditionalism and postmodernism popular among architects. When interwoven with actual historic buildings, or romantically applied to their restoration, Caribbean-style thus becomes, "more fantasy than homage," while also seriously eroding the remaining historic fabric.[20]

Elsewhere, it is not simply the style of building that is changing, but the whole social fabric. In Urbino, Italy, preservation initially focused first on the palace, secondly on the Renaissance. The surrounding region was largely ignored. In the postwar decade, this region experienced dramatic social shifts. Most notable among these shifts was a decline in the percentage of people engaged in agriculture, from 61 percent in 1951 to 10 percent in 1991. State-supported agribusiness has taken over from small farmers. Tourism, industry, and the university are putting new pressures on the landscape. A new preservation plan for Urbino will be regional in nature and will address the needs of protecting the surrounding landscape and of preserving the infrastructure of small towns.[21] But this plan may be locking the barn door after the horse is gone. For, as one critic remarks, considerable displacements have already occurred. "Farmers live in highrises, academics live in farmhouses, and tourists and students live in medieval town houses. The newest monumental forms are microwave relay stations."[22] Similar patterns of displacement can be found throughout Europe's old towns and villages.

In the wake of economic and cultural transformations such as these, the whole issue of authenticity becomes hopelessly clouded. Historic structures may be preserved in a spirit as true to their original form as can be approximated, given the countervailing demands of tourist education, comfort, and safety. But their whole surround becomes problematic, as we robe our very selves in pretense, as we pretend that it is indeed possible to step back in time. One educated Turkish woman related how, on a riverboat tour in the Philippines, she caught a view of the "natives" offstage, relaxing and smoking on the beach. As soon as the boat swung around the bend in the river, the natives put on their act, welcoming the tourists with dances, garlands, and happy smiles. She felt a sense of embarrassment for both them and the tourists for whom this performance was being manufactured.

We have been playing social roles all along. Acting within social constraints, we have cherished the freedom to be our own directors, to choose our own props, speak our own lines, and, in general, manage the impressions we give and give off.[23] To a considerable extent, we have also been free to select the audiences for whom we will perform. Increasingly, strange audiences, speaking foreign languages, dressed in double-knits, and carrying cameras and video recorders, are appearing at our front door to catch us in the act of being ourselves, filled as we are with the discreet charm of the authentic inhabitant.

Conclusion ▨ CHAPTER 9

Getting in Touch with History

Tour historic New Harmony.
Experience a legacy of creative endeavor.
Walk the quiet streets as your guide explains
the history and historic buildings, as well as
the architectural designs of modern masters.
Savor the unmistakable charm of a town
that has held international attention for more
than 175 years.
Set aside some time for New Harmony's
turn-of-the-century shopping area.
—Historic New Harmony, Indiana, brochure

How you feel about preservation depends in part on how you feel about history. Nietzsche spoke of the heaviness of history, of how the sheer volume of the past can weigh on the present. Everything had somehow already been tried: people in the past have already exhausted so many of our possible options. By contrast, novelist Milan Kundera suggests that what people feel today is not the heaviness of history, but an almost "unbearable lightness of being." Everything that occurs threatens to pass away so quickly we are not even sure whether it really happened. We are even less sure if our perceptions of events are shared, a collective phenomenon, or purely individual sensations.[1]

Within the context of preservation, the past can seem either incredibly heavy or incredibly light. The sense that all known patterns of social life were being swept away encouraged early preservationists to mount the Preservation Project and protect historic structures still sacred to the collective memory. As we have seen, however, this collective memory is not uniform across the population. And it does not emerge simply, naturally, from history. Rather it is shaped by status groups who become society's symbolic bankers and whose efforts to preserve sites or artifacts often assume the character of symbolic crusades.

If the past still seems light and likely to slip away if concrete efforts are not made to keep it in mind and in view, the actual cost of maintaining historic remains weighs increasingly heavily. Monuments great and small are being subjected not simply to the ravages of time, but to new forms of destruction, including tourism and pollution. Consciousness of the threat is greater, as recognition of the need to preserve assumes global dimensions. Better research and communication make preservationists in one country better informed about the state and fate of monuments the world over.

In addition to the weight of threatened sites globally, there is the weight of history upon the polity. It has been in the interest of preservationists to widen the range of structures considered worthy of preservation, in terms of both building type and antiquity. A 1950s diner is seen by some as worthy of preservation, depending on its type and condition, as a Saxon church. A process of colonization has occurred, as preservationists have taken over buildings and laid down rules, or at least "guidelines," for their utilization and interpretation.

Unlike the former colonial powers, preservationists are far from having achieved anything like hegemonic control. To some extent, the public can say "No." This is happening in Britain, where stately listed historic homes cannot find buyers willing to spend the money necessary to restore them to their required condition. The result is that the houses fall further into ruin. Buildings with fewer restrictions, industrial row houses, for example, are subject to individual touches—from gnomes to Georgian windows—that preservationists see as ruining the historic streetscape. Britain is now divided between those who feel the heritage industry has expanded beyond all reason and threatens to turn Britain into one great theme park, and those who feel that not enough is being done to protect British treasures or to exploit the potential in heritage tourism.

In America, there is a greater emphasis on pluralism in preservation. This emphasis takes several forms. Preservation professionals stress the importance of grass-roots activism. They also are raising the banner of cultural diversity, seeking to include African-American, Asian-American, and Native-American people among their ranks and to preserve buildings in ethnic neighborhoods.

Yet at the very time that preservation is celebrating amateur activism and cultural diversity, the field is becoming more professionalized and bureaucratized. These divergent conditions leave American preservationists with the conundrum of wanting to share control—because it is the right, pluralistic, American thing to do —and to hold on to control—because they need to maintain their professional status and position in the marketplace. Gnawing away in the back of some minds is that realization that, in contemporary society, all standards are up for question. There is no longer any bedrock of values supporting what preservationists do, or what any of us do.

In this situation, preservationists are unlikely to achieve a public consensus legitimating their project. Their arguments about the public's "right" to beauty, history, light and air, are likely to fall on increasingly deaf ears, especially given economic troubles in Britain and the United States. Preservationists, like most of us, want to do the right thing. But they will not be able to achieve a utopia wherein a perfect class/ethnic/gender mix of professionals and amateurs saves all the right buildings, with the right technology, and for the right reasons. Utopias of social perfection may be appealing in the abstract. In operation, they attempt to by-pass social and political process and to deny class interests.

Instead, these interests and processes are the essential starting points for all social action. Like-minded people join to create projects for social change, for which they then try to gather more widespread support. Some of their arguments may appeal to class interests, but they need also to appeal to the interests of the broader collectivity.[2]

People have collective needs extending beyond individual rights. The collective memory needs to be anchored in visual monuments as well as in works of art and social narratives. There is a need for some measure of social solidarity, even as, or especially as, society becomes more differentiated. Preservation can help respond to this collective need, enabling people to view themselves not simply as individuals, with individual rights, or as members of classes, with opposing interests. Preservation can form local and even national arenas in which people join with others who are different, even strangers, in the complex flow of time. "The earth belongs to the living," said Jefferson. But then he went on to specify that the living held the past in trust for the future.

Preservationists can help develop the sense of solidarity and can reinforce collective memory by identifying and interpreting social markers and by working with communities. But they can never hope to rise above politics, to reach a point where all people worship history at the same shrines and in the same manner. Interpretation will remain political because people have always been political animals and because our collective memories contain elements that are both shared and individual. This much, at least, we learn from history.

NOTES

CHAPTER 1 **The Preservation Project**

Mira Engler, "Drive-Thru History: Theme Towns in Iowa," *Landscape* 32, no. 1 (1993): 9.

1. Karin Knorr-Cettina, *The Manufacture of Knowledge: An Essay on the Constructivist and Contextual Nature of Science* (Elmsford, N.Y.: Pergamon, 1985).
2. Robert Hewison, *The Heritage Industry: Britain in a Climate of Decline* (London: Methuen, 1987).
3. See Patrick Wright, *On Living in an Old Country: The National Past in Contemporary Britain* (London: Verso, 1985).
4. Robin Fedden, *The Continuing Purpose: A History of the National Trust, Its Aims and Work* (London: Longmans, 1968), 79.
5. James Biddle, introduction to National Trust for Historic Preservation, *America's Forgotten Architecture,* ed. Tony P. Wrenn and Elizabeth Mulloy (New York: Pantheon, 1976).
6. Arnold Berke, "Sham in Pasadena: How the World Sees Us," *Historic Preservation News* (May 1991): 4.
7. Hugh Howard, *The Preservationist's Progress: Architectural Adventures in Conserving Yesterday's Houses* (New York: Farrar, Straus and Giroux, 1991), 22. See also David Lowenthal, *The Past is Another Country* (Cambridge: Cambridge University Press, 1985).
8. Maria Stieglitz, "A New Role for a Modernist Landmark," *Historic Preservation News* (November 1992): 13, 29.

CHAPTER 2 **Symbolic Bankers and Cultural Capital**

1. See Paul DiMaggio and Michael Useem, "Social Class and Arts Consumption," *Theory and Society* 5 (1978): 141–161; Judith R. Blau, *The Shape of Culture: A Study of Contemporary Cultural Patterns in the*

United States (Cambridge: Cambridge University Press, 1989); Vera Zolberg, *Constructing a Sociology of the Arts* (Cambridge: Cambridge University Press, 1990); Robert Garfias, "Cultural Diversity and the Arts in America," in *Public Money & the Muse: Essays on Government Funding for the Arts,* ed. Stephen Benedict, (New York: W. W. Norton, 1991), 182–194; and Gerald D. Yoshitomi, "Cultural Democracy," also in Benedict, 195–215.

2. Pierre Bourdieu, *Distinction: A Social Critique of the Judgment of Taste,* trans. Richard Nice (Cambridge: Harvard University Press, 1991). While the concept of cultural capital has been variously defined and elaborated since Bourdieu's seminal work, perhaps the clearest definition, and the most useful for our purposes, is provided by Michele Lamont and Annette Lareau. They define cultural capital as "institutionalized, i.e. widely shared, high status cultural signals (attitudes, preferences, formal knowlege, goods and credentials) used for social and cultural exclusion." The dominant class makes its own cultural preferences and behaviors appear naturally superior to those of the lower classes. Bourdieu and Passeron see this as a form of "symbolic violence," imposing meanings while concealing the underlying power relationship. See Lamont and Lareau, "Cultural Capital: Allusions, Gaps and Glissandos in Recent Theoretical Developments," *Sociological Theory* 6 (fall 1988): 153–168. See also Pierre Bourdieu and Jean-Claude Passeron, *Reproduction in Education, Society and Culture* (Beverly Hills, Calif.: Sage Publications, 1977).

3. Kenneth Burke, *Attitudes Toward History* (Berkeley: University of California Press 1984), 179.

4. Raymond Williams, *Culture and Society, 1780–1950* (New York: Columbia University Press, 1983).

5. Charles Dellheim, *The Face of the Past: The Preservation of the Medieval Inheritance in Victorian England* (Cambridge: Cambridge University Press, 1982), 4.

6. D. M. Matheson, "The Work of the National Trust," *The National Trust: A Record of Fifty Years' Achievement,* ed. J. Lees-Milne (London: B. T. Batsford, 1945), 122–125.

7. John Ruskin, *The Seven Lamps of Architecture* (New York: E. P. Dutton, 1906).

8. Paul Thompson, *The Work of William Morris* (London: Heinemann, 1967), 59.

9. Dellheim, *The Face of the Past,* 46.

10. Fedden, *The Continuing Purpose,* 3.

11. Ibid., 3.

12. Matheson, "The Work of the National Trust," 122.

13. Fedden, *The Continuing Purpose.* Fedden goes on to mention that the group's constitution specified that active membership was "terminable only by death; but (that) this is not so difficult as might be supposed."

14. Ibid.,139.

15. Linda Irvin, ed., *The Encyclopedia of Associations; International Organizations,* 27th ed. (Detroit, Mich.: Gale Research 1992), 699.

16. Fedden, *The Continuing Purpose,* 39.
17. Ibid., 25.
18. Ibid., 39–43.
19. Ibid. See also John Gaze, *Figures in a Landscape: A History of the National Trust* (London: Barrie & Jenkins, 1988).
20. National Trust for Historic Preservation, *America's Forgotten Architecture* (New York: Pantheon, 1976), 21.
21. Charles B. Hosmer, Jr., *Preservation Comes of Age: From Williamsburg to the National Trust, 1926–1949,* 2 vols. (Charlottesville: University of Virginia Press, 1981). See also Michael Kammen, *Mystic Chords of Memory: The Transformation of Tradition in American Culture* (New York: Alfred A. Knopf).
22. Hosmer, *Preservation Comes of Age,* 273.
23. Ibid.
24. This statement, made available to me by the National Trust, was adopted by its Board of Trustees on 14 January 1992.
25. Boston also has a Women's Heritage Trail, comprised of four separate walks which celebrate the struggles and achievements of four centuries of Boston women.
26. Antoinette Lee, "Multicultural Building Blocks," in *Past Meets Future,* ed. Antoinette Lee (Washington, D.C.: The Preservation Press, 1992), 93–97.
27. David Lowenthal, "A Global Perspective on American Heritage", in *Past Meets Future,* 161–162.
28. Thomas W. Sweeney, "Cultural Diversity: An American Tradition," *Historic Preservation News* 32, no. 7 (September 1992): 8.
29. Arnold Berke and Thomas W. Sweeney, "Moving Ahead in Miami," *Historic Preservation News* 32, no. 10 (December 1992): 15.
30. Ibid.
31. See Kenneth Burke, *Attitudes Toward History* (Berkeley: University of California Press, 1984).
32. Hewison, in *The Heritage Industry,* 140.
33. Lowenthal, "A Global Perspective," 159.
34. For a discussion of ethnicity as folklore and as politics, see my chapter on "The Role of Ethnicity" in *Social Standing in America,* ed. Richard P. Coleman and Lee Rainwater (New York: Basic Books, 1978), 92–116.
35. John Urry, *The Tourist Gaze: Leisure and Travel in Contemporary Societies* (Newbury Park, Calif.: Sage Publications, 1990), 144.
36. Geoffrey Scott, *The Architecture of Humanism: A Study in the History of Taste* (New York: Charles Scribner's Sons, 1914).
37. Ann MacEwen and Malcolm MacEwen, *National Parks: Conservation or Cosmetics* (London: Allen & Unwin, 1982).
38. C. Wright Mills, *The Power Elite* (New York: Oxford University Press, 1967).
39. Raymond Williams, *The Country and the City* (New York: Oxford University Press, 1973).
40. Dellheim, *The Face of the Past,* 58.

41. Edward Shils, *Center and Periphery: Essays in Macrosociology* (Chicago: University of Chicago Press, 1975).
42. MacEwen and MacEwen, *National Parks*.
43. Herbert Gans, *Popular Culture and High Culture: An Analysis and Evaluation of Taste* (New York: Basic Books, 1974).
44. Jacques Donzelot, *The Policing of Families*, trans. Robert Hurley (New York: Pantheon, 1979).
45. Fedden, *The Continuing Purpose*, 53.
46. See Bourdieu and Passeron, *Reproduction in Education, Society and Culture*.
47. Joshua C. Taylor, *America as Art* (Washington, D.C.: Smithsonian Institution Press, 1976).
48. Barry Schwartz and Eugene F. Miller, "The Icon and the Word: A Study in the Visual Description of Moral Character," *Semiotica* 6 (1986): 69–99.
49. Hervé Varenne, *Americans Together: Structured Diversity in a Midwestern Town* (New York; Teachers' College Press, 1977).

CHAPTER 3 **Back to Utopia**

Description of Old Bethpage Village Restoration, Long Island, New York, excerpted from the *Old Bethpage Enquirer and Long Island Advertiser* 14, no. 2 (fall 1989): 1.

1. Krishan Kumar, *Utopia and Anti-Utopia in Modern Times* (Oxford: Basil Blackwell, 1987).
2. See George Boas, "Primitivism," *Dictionary of the History of Ideas: Studies of Selected Pivotal Ideas,* ed. Philip P. Wiener, 4 vols. (New York: Charles Scribner's Sons, 1973), 2: 577–598. See also Arthur O. Lovejoy and George Boas, *Primitivism and Related Ideas in Antiquity* (Baltimore: Johns Hopkins University Press, 1935).
3. In labeling such "communities" Staged Symbolic Communities, I am drawing on the work of Gerald Suttles and Albert Hunter, and indirectly on the work of many other community sociologists, as well as scholars interested in the symbolism of space. Suttles has discussed the processes through which communities construct their moral and social order, while Hunter coins the term "symbolic communities" to describe the importance of "shared or collective representations." See Gerald Suttles, *The Social Construction of Communities* (Chicago: University of Chicago Press, 1972) and Albert Hunter, *Symbolic Communities* (Chicago: University of Chicago Press, 1974).

   For a historical overview of open-air museums, see Fredrick Livesay, Joel Lever, and Edith Serkownek, "The Origins of Open-Air Museums," *American Heritage* 9, no. 3 (1993): 4–9. The same issue also contains a historical account of Cooperstown by Leanne Albert, Angelica Docog, Anita Jacobson, et. al., "Spirit of the Past: The Story of the Farmers' Museum," 10–21.
4. Diane Barthel, *Amana: From Pietist Sect to American Community* (Lincoln: University of Nebraska Press, 1984).
5. Ralf Dahrendorf, "Out of Utopia: Toward a Reorientation of Sociolog-

ical Analysis," in *Essays in the Theory of Society* (Stanford: Stanford University Press, l968), 107. On this point of absence of change, see also Louis Marin's consideration of Disneyland as a "degenerate utopia" in his *Utopics: Spatial Play,* trans. Robert A. Vollrath (Atlantic Highlands, N.J.: Humanities Press, 1984).

6. Dahrendorf, "Out of Utopia," 109.

7. Ibid., 110.

8. Thomas J. Schlereth, *Cultural History and Material Culture: Everyday Life, Landscapes, Museums* (Ann Arbor, Mich.: UMI Research Press, 1989).

9. Walter Karp, "Putting Worms Back in Apples," *American Heritage* 33 (1982): 33–43.

10. Charles B. Hosmer, Jr., *Preservation Comes of Age,* 114.

11. For an interesting analysis of a similar phenomenon in Austria, see Adolf W. Ehrentraut, "Heritage Without History: The Open Air Museums of Austria" (paper presented at the Joint International Conference of the Commission for Visual Anthropology, International Visual Sociology Association, Society for Visual Anthropology and other associations, Amsterdam, 1989).

12. This genteel image, while still dominant, is being challenged. At Colonial Williamsburg, for example, slavery has been written back into the narrative. The effort to achieve authenticity carries social risks, however. For example, a 1994 staging of a mock slave auction at Williamsburg drew outrage from African-Americans who considered it degrading and demoralizing. At other sites as well, curators debate how much conflict they can depict without threatening the pleasurable quality of tourist visitations.

13. Sigmund Freud, *Civilization and Its Discontents,* trans. James Strachey (New York: W. W. Norton, 1961).

14. Daniel J. Boorstin, *The Image: A Guide to Pseudo-Events in America* (New York: Atheneum, 1973).

15. Dean MacCannell, *The Tourist: A New Theory of the Leisure Class* (New York: Schocken Books, 1976), 36.

16. Ibid., 62.

17. Thorstein Veblen, *The Theory of the Leisure Class: An Economic Study of Institutions* (New York: B. W. Huebsch, 1919).

18. Jacques Donzelot, *The Policing of Families.*

19. Roland Barthes, *The Pleasure of the Text,* trans. Richard Miller (New York: Hill & Wang, 1975).

20. Tania Modleski, *Loving with a Vengeance: Mass-Produced Fantasies for Women* (New York: Methuen, 1982).

21. Jean-François Lyotard, *The Postmodern Condition: A Report on Knowledge,* trans. Geoff Bennington and Brian Massumi (Manchester: University of Manchester Press, 1986).

22. Ronald Lee Fleming, "A Tale of Two Villages," *Places* 7, no. 3 (n.d.): 36–45.

23. MacCannell, *The Tourist.*

24. Ibid.

25. Barthel, *Amana,* 152.
26. William Butler, "Another City Upon a Hill: Litchfield, Connecticut, and the Colonial Revival," in *The Colonial Revival in America,* ed. Alan Axelrod (New York: W. W. Norton, 1985), 15–51.
27. Herbert Gans, *The Levittowners* (New York: Random House, 1967), 145.
28. Ibid.
29. J. R. Seeley, R. A. Sim, and E. W. Loosley, *Crestwood Heights* (New York: Wiley, 1963).
30. Raymond Williams, *Resources of Hope: Culture, Democracy, Socialism,* ed. Robert Gable (London: Verso, 1989).
31. Alan Axelrod, *The Colonial Revival in America.*
32. Hugh Lloyd-Jones, *The Justice of Zeus* (Berkeley: University of California Press, 1983).
33. Stephen Thernstrom, "Yankee City Revisited: The Perils of Historical Naïveté," *American Sociological Review* 30 (1965): 234–242.
34. Barthel, Amana.
35. John Brinckerhoff Jackson, *The Necessity for Ruins and Other Topics* (Amherst: University of Massachusetts Press, 1980).
36. "Sparks Fly in Catskills over Fantasyland Plan," *New York Times,* Monday, 3 April 1989, p. B2.
37. David Mohney and Keller Easterling, *Seaside: Making a Town in America* (Princeton: Princeton University Press, 1989).
38. Craig Jackson Calhoun, "The Radicalism of Tradition: Community Strength or Venerable Disguise and Borrowed Language," *American Journal of Sociology* 88 (1983): 886–914.

CHAPTER 4 *The Interpretation of Industrial Society*

1. See for example Daniel Bell, *The Coming of Post-Industrial Society: A Venture in Social Forecasting* (London: Heinemann, 1974); Douglas Kellner, *Critical Theory, Marxism, and Modernity* (Baltimore: Johns Hopkins University Press, 1989).
2. See Daniel J. Boorstin, *The Republic of Technology: Reflections on Our Future Community* (New York: Harper & Row, 1978); John F. Kasson, *Civilizing the Machine: Technology and Republican Values in America, 1776–1900* (New York: Penguin, 1976); Leo Marx, *The Machine in the Garden: Technology and the Pastoral Ideal in America* (New York: Oxford University Press, 1964); Lewis Mumford, *Technics and Civilization* (New York: Harcourt, Brace and Co., 1934); Witold Rybczynski, *Taming the Tiger: The Struggle to Control Technology* (New York: Viking Press, 1983).
3. J.P.M. Pannell, *The Techniques of Industrial Archaeology* (Newton Abbot, Devon: David & Charles, 1974).
4. Dellheim, *The Face of the Past;* William Cobbett, *Rural Rides* (Baltimore: Penguin 1967); Thomas Carlyle, *Past and Present* (New York: Charles Scribner's Sons, 1918).
5. Architectural firm of Venturi, Rauch and Scott Brown, cited in John F.

Sears, *Sacred Places: American Tourist Attractions in the Nineteenth Century* (New York: Oxford University Press, 1989), 208.

6. The Reader's Digest Association, *Discovering Britain: Where to See the Best of Our Countryside* (London: Drive Publications, 1982), 33.

7. Tamara Hareven, *Amoskeag* (New York: Pantheon, 1978).

8. The literature on museums is substantial and growing. See for example Ivan Karp and Steven D. Lavine, *Exhibiting Cultures: The Poetics and Politics of Museum Display* (Washington, D.C.: Smithsonian Institution Press, 1991); Douglas Davis, *The Museum Transformed: Design and Culture in the Post-Pompidou Age* (New York: Abbeville Press, 1990), Robert Lumley, ed., *The Museum Time-Machine: Putting Cultures on Display* (New York: Routledge, 1988); and George W. Stocking, Jr., ed., *Objects and Others: Essays on Museums and Material Culture* (Madison: University of Wisconsin Press, 1985).

9. Alan Morton, "Tomorrow's Yesterdays: Science Museums and the Future," in *The Museum Time-Machine,* 128–143.

10. Hosmer, *Preservation Comes of Age.*

11. Marx, *Machine in the Garden.*

12. Burke, *Attitudes Toward History.*

13. Peter Maris, *Loss and Change* (New York: Pantheon, 1974).

14. Kenneth Hudson, *Handbook for Industrial Archaeologists: A Guide to Fieldwork and Research* (London: John Baker, 1967), 3.

15. U. S. Department of the Interior, "Hopewell Furnace: A Guide to Hopewell Furnace National Historic Site, Pennsylvania" (Washington, D.C.: National Park Service Division of Publications, 1983), 24.

16. Jackson, *The Necessity for Ruins.* See also Barry Schwartz, "Social Change and Collective Memory: The Democratization of George Washington," *American Sociological Review* 56 (1991): 221–236.

17. Anthony Burton, *Remains of a Revolution* (London: Andre Deutsch, 1983), 9.

18. Max Horkheimer, and Theodor W. Adorno, *Dialectic of Enlightenment,* trans. John Cumming (New York: Continuum, 1986), Stanley Aronowitz, *Science as Power: Discourse and Ideology in Modern Society* (Minneapolis: University of Minnesota Press, 1988); and Raymond Boudon, *The Analysis of Ideology,* trans. Malcolm Slater (Chicago: University of Chicago Press, 1989).

19. Sigmund Freud, *Civilization and Its Discontents,* trans. James Strachey (New York: W. W. Norton, 1961).

20. Roger Neustadter, "The Politics of Growing Up: The Status of Childhood in Modern Social Thought," in *Current Perspectives in Social Theory,* ed. John Wilson (Greenwich, Conn.: JAI Press, 1989), 9: 199–221.

21. Burton, *Remains of a Revolution,* 10.

22. Michael Stratton, "Integrating Technological and Social History: 'Engines of Change' at the National Museum of American History," *Technology and Culture* 31, no. 20 (April 1990): 274.

23. Bob West, "The Making of the English Working Past: A Critical View of the Ironbridge Gorge Museum," in *The Museum Time-Machine,* 36–62.

24. Ibid., 58.
25. Bourdieu and Passeron, *Reproduction in Education.*
26. Michael Brewster Folsom, "The New Social History and the Captains of Industry: Will the Real Nathan Appleton Please Stand Up?" in *The Popular Perception of Industrial History,* ed. Robert Weible and Francis R. Walsh (Lanham, Md.: American Association for State and Local History Library, 1989), 113–121.
27. Bernard S. Finn, "Exhibit Reviews—Twenty Years After," *Technology and Culture* 30 (1989): 991.
28. Carolyn C. Cooper, "The Ghost in the Kitchen: Household Technology at the Brattleboro Museum, Vermont," *Technology and Culture* 28 (1987): 330. On the broader issues involved in evaluating historical changes in women's work, see Ruth Schwartz Cowan, *More Work for Mother: The Ironies of Household Technology from the Open Hearth to the Microwave* (New York: Basic Books, 1983).
29. Geoffrey Tweedale, "Steel Metropolis: A View of Sheffield Industry at Kelham Island Industrial Museum," *Technology and Culture* 33, no. 2 (1992): 334.
30. MacCannell, *The Tourist.*
31. Peter Liebhold, "The Working People of Richmond: Life and Labor in an Industrial City, 1865–1920 at the Valentine Museum, Richmond, Virginia," *Technology and Culture* 33, no. 3 (1992): 569–570.
32. U. S. Department of the Interior, "Hopewell Furnace," 25.
33. Eugene S. Ferguson, "Technical Museums and International Exhibitions," *Technology and Culture* 6 (1965): 46.

CHAPTER 5   *War and Remembrance*

1. On the significance of sacrifice to social solidarity see Emile Durkheim, *The Elementary Forms of Religious Life,* trans. Joseph Ward Swain (New York: Free Press, 1965); George Bataille, *Visions of Excess: Selected Writings, 1927–1939,* ed. Allan Stoekl, trans. Allan Stoekl with Carl R. Lovitt and Donald M. Leslie, Jr. (Manchester: Manchester University Press, 1985); Peter Maris, *Loss and Change;* Maurice Halbwachs, *Les cadres sociaux de la mémoire* (New York: Arno Press, 1975); and Robert Wuthnow, *Meaning and Moral Order: Explorations in Cultural Analysis* (Berkeley: University of California Press, 1987).
2. See Mira Engler, "Drive-Thru History."
3. Jane Brown Gillette, "Fields Unforgotten," *Historic Preservation* 45, no. 4 (July–August 1993): 35–39, 86.
4. "Souvenirs of Gulf War Find Way to Museums," *New York Times,* Tuesday, 28 May 1991, p. A16.
5. Ibid.
6. Douglas Martin, "Tourists, the Peacetime Target of a Shipful of Military Magic," *New York Times,* Friday, 10 January 1992, p. C1.
7. (no author), *Cincinnati Goes to War: A Community Responds to World War II* (Cincinnati: The Cincinnati Historical Society, 1991), 970.

8. Studs Terkel, *"The Good War": An Oral History of World War Two* (New York: Pantheon, 1984).

9. Stephen Kinzer, "The Baring of Buchenwald, Unfettered," *New York Times,* 20 March 1991, p. A3.

10. Michal McMahon, "The Romance of Technological Progress: A Critical Review of the National Air and Space Museum," *Technology and Culture* 22 (1981): 281–296.

11. Martin Walker, "Custer Loses the Last Stand Again," *Manchester Guardian Weekly,* 5 May 1991, 9.

12. Gaye Tuchman, Arlene Kaplan Daniels, and James Benet, eds., *Hearth and Home: Images of Women in the Mass Media* (New York: Oxford University Press, 1978).

13. "Woman Sues Over Exclusion From Events at National Park," *New York Times,* Friday, 25 February 1991, p. B8.

14. These goals are set forward in the visitors' guide to the IWM.

15. Alvin W. Gouldner, *The Dialectic of Ideology and Technology: The Origins, Grammar and Future of Ideology* (New York: Macmillan, 1976).

16. Geoffrey Galt Harpham, *On the Grotesque: Strategies of Contradiction in Art and Literature* (Princeton: Princeton University Press, 1982), 3.

17. Mann cited in Harpham, *On the Grotesque,* xix.

18. Philip Gourevitch, "Behold Now Behemoth," *Harper's Magazine* 87, no. 1718 (1993): 60.

19. All of these issues were raised when German archaeologists uncovered a Nazi bunker in Berlin that SS soldiers had decorated wtih a series of bizarre, sexually titillating frescoes. See Adrian Bridges, "Facing Up to the Past," *The Independent Magazine* 206 (15 August 1992): 40–41.

CHAPTER 6 *Religious Preservation in Secular Society*

1. For an overview of the debates surrounding secularization, see Wolfgang Schluchter, *Rationalism, Religion, and Domination: A Weberian Perspective,* trans. Neil Solomon (Berkeley: University of California Press, 1989).

2. See Durkheim, *The Elementary Forms of the Religious Life.*

3. Ibid.

4. Daniel Bell, "The Return of the Sacred? The Argument on the Future of Religion," in *The Winding Passage: Essays and Sociological Journeys 1960–1980* (New York: Basic Books, 1980), 349.

5. Ibid., 350.

6. Andrew Abbott, *The System of Professions: An Essay on the Division of Expert Labor* (Chicago: University of Chicago Press, 1988).

7. Rachel S. Cox, "Saving Grace," *Historical Preservation* 40 (September-October 1988): 35.

8. Almost 150 people came to celebrate the synagogue's reopening in an ecumenical service, which was followed by a separate ceremony of religious rededication.

9. Robert Bellah, *Beyond Belief: Essays on Religion in a Post-Traditional World* (New York: Harper & Row, 1970).
10. Thomas W. Sweeney, "Parishioners Raise Funds to Save Chicago Church," *Historic Preservation News* (February 1991): 17.
11. Ibid.
12. Asa Briggs, *Victorian Cities* (New York: Harper & Row, 1965).
13. Information provided by the Redundant Churches Fund.
14. Quoted in Martin Wainwright, "Heritage Advisers Revolt against Sites Disposal," *Manchester Guardian Weekly*, 8 November 1992, 4.
15. John Ruskin, *Seven Lamps of Architecture*, chapter 6, entry no. 18 in *Ruskin Today*, ed. Kenneth Clark (Harmondsworth: Penguin, 1965), 249.
16. Ada Louis Huxtable, *Kicked a Building Lately?* (New York: Quadrangle, 1976), 234.
17. David Lowenthal, "Conserving the Heritage: Anglo-American Comparisons," in *The Expanding City* (London: Academic Press, 1983).
18. George Duby, *The Age of the Great Cathedrals: Art and Society 980–1420*, trans. Eleanor Lerieux and Barbara Thompson (London: Croom Helm, 1981).
19. Walter Schwarz, "Ely Puts Its Price on Vision," *Manchester Guardian Weekly*, 11 August 1991, p. 5.
20. Walter Schwarz, "Temporal Leak Fails to Cloud Spiritual View," *Manchester Guardian Weekly*, 1 September 1991, 25.
21. Walter Schwarz, "Cash Counts as Winchester's Saving Grace," *Manchester Guardian Weekly*, 18 August 1991, 26.
22. "Bishop Condemns Cathedral Plan," *Manchester Guardian Weekly*, 27 October 1991, 4.
23. See Joanna Coles, "Plight of the Holy-Owned Subsidiaries," *Manchester Guardian Weekly*, 4 November 1990, 21.
24. Paul Goldberger, *On the Rise: Architecture and Design in a Postmodern Age* (New York: Times Books, 1983), 240.
25. Ibid., 237.
26. Linda Greenhouse, "Court Ends Tower Plan at St. Barts," *New York Times*, Tuesday, 5 March 1991, p. B4.
27. James M. McCown, letter to the editor, *New York Times*, Sunday, 7 April 1991, p. H6.
28. Paul Goldberger, "Two Reasons for Dancing in the Streets of New York," *New York Times*, Sunday, 17 March 1991, p. H36.

CHAPTER 7 *Consuming History*

1. "Unnatural Treasures," *Nature Conservancy* (May/June 1991): 26.
2. Susan Hegeman, "Shopping for Identities: 'A Nation of Nations' and the Weak Ethnicity of Objects," *Public Culture* 3, no. 2 (spring 1991): 71–92.
3. The *Star Trek* exhibit affirmed the importance of the television audience. A special section devoted to "the fans" described the creation and activities of Trekkies. As a media movement, they made history.
4. Carol Vogel, "Bric-a-Brac Revisited: Not a Tag Sale," *New York Times*,

Thursday, 7 November 1991, pp. C1, C10.

5. William E. Schmidt, "Just as in the Dreams, They Come to the Fields," *New York Times,* Thursday, 16 August 1990, p. A18.

6. Harvey Molotch, "The City as a Growth Machine," *American Journal of Sociology* 82, no. 2 (1976): 309–330.

7. Eloise Salholz, with Ann McDaniel and Rich Thomas, "The Anatomy of Pork," *Newsweek,* 13 April 1992, 25.

8. See Martin Walker, "Raising the Stakes in a Bid to Develop Deadwood," *Manchester Guardian Weekly,* 8 March 1992, 21.

9. Erica Browne, "Vandals Ruin Ellis Island Honor Wall," *New York Post,* Saturday, 30 March 1991, 5.

10. Orin Lehman, "Striking a Balance," *New York Times,* Saturday, 24 January 1992, 22.

11. Mike Featherstone, *Postmodernism and Consumer Culture* (Newbury Park, Calif.: Sage Publications, 1991). See also Edward W. Soja, *Postmodern Geographics: A Reassertion of Space in Criticial Social Theory* (London: Verso, 1989); David Harvey, *The Condition of Postmodernity: An Enquiry into the Origins of Cultural Change* (London: Basil Blackwell, 1989); and Sharon Zukin, *Landscapes of Power: From Detroit to Disney World* (Berkeley: University of California Press, 1991).

12. "Facts About the National Trust's National Main Street Center" (Washington, D.C.: National Trust for Historic Preservation, 1993.)

13. Barbara Flanagan, "A Cape Cod Mall is Disappeared," *New York Times,* Thursday, 14 March 1991, p. C10.

14. Ibid.

15. Ibid.

16. Nicolas R. Spitzer, *Ybor City Folk Festival Site Visit Report, Nov. 13–15, 1987* (Washington, D.C.: National Endowment for the Arts, Folk Life Program), 5. Cited in Susan B. Greenbaum, "Marketing Ybor City: Race, Ethnicity, and Historic Preservation in the Sunbelt," *City & Society* 4, no. 1 (June 1990): 74.

17. For the classic theoretical statement, see Walter Benjamin, "The Work of Art in An Age of Mechanical Reproduction," in his *Illuminations,* ed. Hannah Arendt, trans. Harry Zohn (New York: Schocken Books, 1969), 217–251.

18. Also unnerving, for different reasons, is the adoption of Nazi insignia, clothing, gestures, behaviors, and values by disaffected youth. Perhaps no other social current shows how clearly retro styles can represent a perverse reaction to one's time and place, whether on an individual or group basis.

CHAPTER 8 *We Are the World*

ICOMOS News 3, no. 1 (March 1993): 20–23.

1. See Andrej Smrekar and Stane Bernik, "Targeting Croatia's Culture is War Crime," *New York Times,* 28 October 1991, p. A16. The report is

confirmed by Kathleen V. Wilkes, an Oxford University professor who lived in Dubrovnik during the last four months of 1991. See Wilkes, "Historic Dubrovnik Blasted by War," *Historic Preservation News* (February 1991): 15.

2. Andrea Oppenheimer Dean, "On Top of the World," *Historic Preservation* 44, no. 2 (March/April 1992): 40–43, 89.

3. For a discussion of this tension between professional cultures and national governments, particularly as it affects architecture, see Anthony King, "Architecture, Capital and the Globalization of Culture," *Theory Culture & Society* 7, no. 2–3 (June 1990): 397–411.

4. Lowenthal, "A Global Perspective," 158.

5. Peter C. T. Elsworth, "Too Many People and Not Enough Places to Go," *New York Times,* Sunday, 26 May 1991, p. F4.

6. Dennis Johnson, "Shakespearean Theme Park-Upon-Avon," *Manchester Guardian Weekly,* 25 October 1992, 22.

7. "Sights for Sour Eyes," *Manchester Guardian Weekly,* 1 November 1992, 25.

8. David Nicholson-Lord, "Death by Tourism," *The Independent,* 5 August 1990, 5.

9. Ibid., 3.

10. Martin Walker, "Disneyification of the Planet," *Manchester Guardian Weekly,* 4 August 1991, 21.

11. Michael McNay, "Taking the Mickey," *Manchester Guardian Weekly,* November 3, 1991, 29.

12. Deyan Sudjic, "Less Than Wonderful World of Disney," *Manchester Guardian Weekly,* 15 March 1992, 24.

13. For a perceptive analysis of the significance of the Disney theme parks for the American social landscape, see Sharon Zukin's *Landscapes of Power: From Detroit to Disney World.*

14. "Overheard" column, *Newsweek,* 24 June 1991, 15.

15. Andrea Oppenheimer Dean, "Catalytic Converters," *Historic Preservation* (July/August 1992): 15.

16. The former Soviet regime demonstrated a range of attitudes toward historic preservation over the course of its seventy-four-year history. For a brief survey, see Richa Wilson, "The Purpose of the Past," *Places* 8, no. 1 (summer 1992): 46–57.

17. Cherilyn Widell, "Cultural Hurdles for Adaptive Re-Use of Historic Buildings in Japan," *Places* 8, no. 1 (summer 1992): 80–82.

18. Cathy Tuttle, "Buddhist Priests 2: Developers 1," *Places* 8, no. 1 (summer 1992): 82–83.

19. *New York Times,* Thursday, 15 August 1991, p. B20.

20. William R. Chapman, "A Litle More Gingerbread: Tourism, Design, and Preservation in the Caribbean," *Places* 8, no. 1 (summer 1992): 58–67.

21. David Vanderburgh, "Planning, Preservation and Polyculture," *Places* 8, no. 1 (summer 1992): 32–41.

22. Ibid., 32

23. Erving Goffman, *The Presentation of Self in Everyday Life,* (Garden City, N.Y.: Doubleday, 1959).

CHAPTER 9   *Conclusion: Getting in Touch with History*

1. Friedrich Nietzsche, *The Portable Nietzsche*, ed. Walter Kaufmann (New York: Viking, 1954),112–439; Milan Kundera, *The Unbearable Lightness of Being*, trans. Michael H. Heim (New York: Harper and Row, 1987).
2. Alvin W. Gouldner, *The Dialectic of Ideology and Technology.*

REFERENCES

Abbott, A. 1988. *The System of Professions: An Essay on the Division of Expert Labor.* Chicago: University of Chicago Press.

Albert, L., A. Docog, A. Jacobson, et. al. 1993. "Spirit of the Past: The Story of the Farmers' Museum." *American Heritage* 9 (3): 10–21.

Aronowitz, S. 1988. *Science as Power: Discourse and Ideology in Modern Society.* Minneapolis: University of Minnesota Press.

Axelrod, A. 1985. *The Colonial Revival in America.* New York: W. W. Norton.

Barthel, D. 1978. "The Role of Ethnicity." In *Social Standing in America.* Edited by R. Coleman and L. Rainwater. New York: Basic Books.

———. 1984. *Amana: From Pietist Sect to American Community.* Lincoln: University of Nebraska Press.

Bataille, G. 1985. *Visions of Excess: Selected Writings, 1927–1939.* Edited by A. Stoekl, trans. by A. Stoekl with Carl R. Lovitt and Donald M. Leslie, Jr. Manchester: Manchester University Press.

Bell, D. 1974. *The Coming of Post-Industrial Society: A Venture in Social Forecasting.* London: Heinemann.

———. 1980. "The Return of the Sacred? The Argument on the Future of Religion." In *The Winding Passage: Essays and Sociological Journeys 1960–1980.* New York: Basic Books, 1980.

Bellah, R. 1970. *Beyond Belief: Essays on Religion in a Post-Traditional World.* New York: Harper & Row.

Benjamin, W. 1969. "The Work of Art in an Age of Mechanical Reproduction." In *Illuminations,* edited by H. Arendt, trans. by H. Zohn. New York: Schocken Books.

Blau, J. R. 1989. *The Shape of Culture: A Study of Contemporary Cultural Patterns in the United States.* Cambridge: Cambridge University Press.

Boorstin, D. J. 1973. *The Image: A Guide to Pseudo-Events in America.* New York: Atheneum.

———. 1978. *The Republic of Technology: Reflections on Our Future*

Community. New York: Harper & Row.

Boudon, R. 1989. *The Analysis of Ideology.* Trans. by M. Slater. Chicago: University of Chicago Press.

Bourdieu, P. 1991. *Distinction: A Social Critique of the Judgement of Taste.* Trans. by R. Nice. Cambridge: Harvard University Press.

Bourdieu, P. and J.-C. Passeron. 1977. *Reproduction in Education, Society and Culture.* Beverly Hills: Sage Publications.

Briggs, A. 1965. *Victorian Cities.* New York: Harper & Row.

Burke, K. 1984. *Attitudes toward History.* Berkeley: University of California Press.

Burton, A. 1983. *Remains of a Revolution.* London: Andre Deutsch.

Butler, W. 1967. "Another City upon a Hill: Litchfield, Connecticut, and the Colonial Revival." In *The Colonial Revival in America,* edited by A. Axelrod. New York: W. W. Norton.

Calhoun, C. J. 1983. "The Radicalism of Tradition: Community Strength or Venerable Disguise and Borrowed Language." *American Journal of Sociology* 88:886–914.

Carlyle, T. 1918. *Past and Present.* New York: Charles Scribner's Sons.

Chapman, W. R. 1992. "A Little More Gingerbread: Tourism, Design, and Preservation in the Caribbean." *Places* 8 (1): 58–67.

Cobbett, W. 1967 (1830). *Rural Rides.* Baltimore, Md.: Penguin.

Cooper, C. 1987. "The Ghost in the Kitchen: Household Technology at the Brattleboro Museum, Vermont." *Technology and Culture* 28:330.

Cowan, R. S. 1983. *More Work for Mother: The Ironies of Household Technology from the Open Hearth to the Microwave.* New York: Basic Books.

Cox, R. S. 1988. "Saving Grace." *Historic Preservation* 40:34–38.

Dahrendorf, R. 1968. "Out of Utopia: Toward a Reorientation of Sociological Analysis." In *Essays in the Theory of Society.* Stanford: Stanford University Press.

Davis, D. 1990. *The Museum Transformed: Design and Culture in the Post-Pompidou Age.* New York: Abbeville Press.

Dean, A. O. 1992. "On Top of the World." *Historic Preservation* 44 (2): 40–43, 89.

Dellheim, C. 1982. *The Face of the Past: The Preservation of the Medieval Inheritance in Victorian England.* Cambridge: Cambridge University Press.

DiMaggio, P., and M. Useem. 1978. "Social Class and Arts Consumption." *Theory and Society* 5:141–161.

Donzelot, J. 1979. *The Policing of Families.* Trans. by R. Hurley. New York: Pantheon.

Duby, G. 1981. *The Age of the Great Cathedrals: Art and Society 980–1420.* Trans. by E. Lerieux and B. Thompson. London: Croom Helm.

Durkheim, E. 1965. *The Elementary Forms of Religious Life.* Trans. by J. W. Swain. New York: Free Press.

Ehrentraut, A. 1989. "Heritage without History: The Open Air Museums of Austria." Paper presented at the Joint International Conference of the Commission for Visual Anthropology, International Visual Sociology

Association, Society for Visual Anthropology and other associations, Amsterdam.

Engler, M. 1993. "Drive-Thru History: Theme Towns in Iowa." *Landscape* 32 (1): 8–18.

Featherstone, M. 1991. *Postmodernism and Consumer Culture.* Newbury Park, Calif.: Sage Publications.

Fedden, R. 1968. *The Continuing Purpose: A History of the National Trust, Its Aims and Work.* London: Longmans.

Ferguson, E. S. 1965. "Technical Museums and International Exhibitions." *Technology and Culture* 6:30–46.

Finn, B. 1987. "Exhibit Reviews—Twenty Years After." *Technology and Culture* 30:993–1003.

Fleming, R. L. n.d. "A Tale of Two Villages." *Places* 7 (3): 36–45.

Folsom, M. B. 1989. "The New Social History and the Captains of Industry: Will the Real Nathan Appleton Please Stand Up?" In *The Popular Perception of Industrial History,* edited by R. Weible and F. R. Walsh. Lanham, Md.: American Association for State and Local History Library.

Freud, S. 1961. *Civilization and Its Discontents.* Trans. by J. Strachey. New York: W. W. Norton.

Gans, H. 1967. *The Levittowners.* New York: Random House.

———. 1974. *Popular Culture and High Culture: An Analysis and Evaluation of Taste.* New York: Basic Books.

Garfias, R. 1991. "Cultural Diversity and the Arts in America." In *Public Money & the Muse: Essays on Government Funding for the Arts.* New York: W. W. Norton.

Gaze, J. 1988. *Figures in a Landscape: A History of the National Trust.* London: Barrie & Jenkins.

Gillette, J. B. 1993. "Fields Unforgotten." *Historic Preservation* 45 (4): 35–39, 86.

Goffman, E. 1959. *The Presentation of Self in Everyday Life.* Garden City, N.Y.: Doubleday.

Goldberger, P. 1983. *On the Rise: Architecture and Design in a Postmodern Age.* New York: Times Books.

Gouldner, A. W. 1976. *The Dialectic of Ideology and Technology: The Origins, Grammar and Future of Ideology.* New York: Macmillan.

Gourevitch, P. 1993. "Behold Now Behemoth." *Harper's Magazine* 87:55–62.

Greenbaum, S. 1990. "Marketing Ybor City: Race, Ethnicity, and Historic Preservation in the Sunbelt." *City & Society* 4 (1): 58–76.

Halbwachs, M. 1975. *Les cadres sociaux de la mémoire.* New York: Arno Press.

Hareven, T. 1978. *Amoskeag.* New York: Pantheon.

Harpham, G. G. 1982. *On the Grotesque: Strategies of Contradiction in Art and Literature.* Princeton: Princeton University Press.

Harvey, D. 1989. *The Condition of Postmodernity: An Enquiry into the Origins of Cultural Change.* London: Basil Blackwell.

Hegeman, S. 1991. "Shopping for Identities: 'A Nation of Nations' and the Weak Ethnicity of Objects." *Public Culture* 3 (2): 71–92.

Hewison, R. 1987. *The Heritage Industry: Britain in a Climate of Decline.*

London: Methuen.

Horkheimer, M. and T. W. Adorno. 1986. *Dialectic of Enlightenment.* Trans. by J. Cumming. New York: Continuum.

Hosmer, C. B. Jr. 1981. *Preservation Comes of Age: From Williamsburg to the National Trust, 1926–1949.* Charlottesville: University of Virginia Press.

Howard, H. 1991. *The Preservationist's Progress: Architectural Adventures in Conserving Yesterday's Houses.* New York: Farrar, Straus and Giroux.

Hudson, K. 1967. *Handbook for Industrial Archaeologists: A Guide to Fieldwork and Research.* London: John Baker.

Hunter, A. 1974. *Symbolic Communities.* Chicago: University of Chicago Press.

Huxtable, A. L. 1976. *Kicked a Building Lately?* New York: Quadrangle.

Kammen, M. 1991. *Mystic Chords of Memory: The Transformation of Tradition in American Culture.* New York: Alfred A. Knopf.

Karp, I. and S. D. Lavine. 1991. *Exhibiting Cultures: The Poetics and Politics of Museum Display.* Washington, D.C.: Smithsonian Press.

Karp, W. 1982. "Putting Worms Back in Apples." *American Heritage* 33:33–43.

Kasson, J. F. 1976. *Civilizing the Machine: Technology and Republican Values in America, 1776–1900.* New York: Penguin.

Kellner, D. 1989. *Critical Theory, Marxism, and Modernity.* Baltimore: Johns Hopkins University Press.

King, A. 1990. "Architecture, Capital and the Globalization of Culture." *Theory, Culture & Society* 7:397–411.

Knorr-Cettina, K. 1985. *The Manufacture of Knowledge: An Essay on the Constructivist and Contextual Nature of Science.* Elmsford, N.Y.: Pergamon.

Kumar, K. 1987. *Utopia and Anti-Utopia in Modern Times.* Oxford: Basil Blackwell.

Kundera, M. 1987. *The Unbearable Lightness of Being.* Trans. by M. H. Heim. New York: Harper and Row.

Jackson, J. B. 1980. *The Necessity for Ruins and Other Topics.* Amherst: University of Massachusetts Press.

Lamont, M., and A. Lareau. 1988. "Cultural Capital: Allusions, Gaps and Glissandos in Recent Theoretical Developments." *Sociological Theory* 6:153–168.

Lee, A. 1992. "Multicultural Building Blocks." In *Past Meets Future,* edited by A. Lee. Washington, D.C.: The Preservation Press.

Liebhold, P. 1992. "The Working People of Richmond: Life and Labor in an Industrial City, 1865–1920 at the Valentine Museum, Richmond, Virginia." *Technology and Culture* 33:569–570.

Livesay, F., J. Lever, and E. Serkownek. 1993. "The Origins of Open-Air Museums." *American Heritage* 9 (3): 4–9.

Lloyd-Jones, H. 1983. *The Justice of Zeus.* Berkeley: University of California Press.

Lowenthal, D. 1983. "Conserving the Heritage: Anglo-American Comparisons." In *The Expanding City: Essays in Honour of Jean Gottmann,* edited by John Patten. London: Academic Press.

———. 1985. *The Past is a Foreign Country.* Cambridge: Cambridge University Press.

———. 1992. "A Global Perspective on American Heritage." In *Past Meets Future,* by A. Lee.

Lowenthal, D., and M. Binney, eds. 1987. *Our Past before Us.* London: Temple Smith.

Lumley, R., ed. 1988. *The Museum Time-Machine: Putting Cultures on Display.* New York: Routledge.

Lyotard, J.-F. 1986. *The Postmodern Condition: A Report on Knowledge.* Trans. by G. Bennington and B. Massumi. Manchester: University of Manchester Press.

MacCannell, D. 1976. *The Tourist: A New Theory of the Leisure Class.* New York: Schocken Books.

MacEwen, A., and M. MacEwen. 1982. *National Parks: Conservation or Cosmetics.* London: Allen & Unwin.

McMahon, M. 1981. "The Romance of Technological Progress: A Critical Review of the National Air and Space Museum." *Technology and Culture* 22:281–296.

Maris, P. 1974. *Loss and Change.* New York: Pantheon.

Marx, L. 1964. *The Machine in the Garden: Technology and the Pastoral Ideal in America.* New York: Oxford University Press.

Matheson, D. M.1945. "The Work of the National Trust." In *The National Trust: A Record of Fifty Years' Achievement,* edited by J. Lees-Milne. London: B. T. Batsford.

Modleski, T. 1982. *Loving with a Vengeance: Mass-Produced Fantasies for Women.* New York: Methuen.

Mohney, D. and K. Easterling. 1989. *Seaside: Making a Town in America.* Princeton: Princeton University Press.

Molotch, H. 1976. "The City as a Growth Machine." *American Journal of Sociology* 82 (2): 309–330.

Morton, A. "Tomorrow's Yesterdays: Science Museums and the Future." In *The Museum Time-Machine: Putting Culture on Display,* edited by R. Lumley. London: Routledge.

Mumford, L. 1934. *Technics and Civilization.* New York: Harcourt, Brace and Co.

National Trust for Historic Preservation, 1976. *America's Forgotten Architecture.* Edited by T. P. Wrenn and E. Mulloy. New York: Pantheon.

Neustadter, R. 1989. "The Politics of Growing Up: The Status of Childhood in Modern Social Thought." In *Current Perspectives in Social Theory,* vol. 9, edited by J. Wilson. Greenwich, Conn.: JAI Press.

Nietzsche, F. 1954. *The Portable Nietzsche.* Edited by W. Kaufmann. New York: Viking.

Pannell, J.P.M. *The Techniques of Industrial Archaeology.* Newton Abbot, Devon: David & Charles.

Reader's Digest Association. 1982. *Discovering Britain: Where to See the Best of Our Countryside.* London: Drive Publications.

Ruskin, J. 1906. *The Seven Lamps of Architecture.* New York: E. P. Dutton.

Rybczynski, W. 1983. *Taming the Tiger: The Struggle to Control Technology.* New York: Viking Press.

Schlereth, T. J. 1989. *Cultural History and Material Culture: Everyday Life, Landscapes, Museums.* Ann Arbor, Mich.: UMI Reserach Press.

Schluchter, W. 1989. *Rationalism, Religion, and Domination: A Weberian Perspective.* Berkeley: University of California Press.

Schwartz, B. 1991. "Social Change and Collective Memory: The Democratization of George Washington." *American Sociological Review* 56:221–236.

Schwartz, B., and E. F. Miller. 1986. "The Icon and the Word: A Study in the Visual Description of Moral Character." *Semiotica* 6:69–99.

Scott, G. 1914. *The Architecture of Humanism: A Study in the History of Taste.* New York: Charles Scribner's Sons.

Sears, J. F. 1989. *Sacred Places: American Tourist Attractions in the Nineteenth Century.* New York: Oxford University Press.

Seeley, J. R., R. A. Sim, and E. W. Loosley. 1963. *Crestwood Heights.* New York: Wiley.

Shils, E. 1975. *Center and Periphery: Essays in Macrosociology.* Chicago: University of Chicago Press.

Soja, E. A. 1989. *Postmodern Geographies: A Reassertion of Space in Critical Theory.* London: Verso.

Stocking, G. W., Jr., ed. 1985. *Objects and Others: Essays on Museums and Material Culture.* Madison: University of Wisconsin Press.

Stratton, M. 1990. "Integrating Technological and Social History: 'Engines of Change' at the National Museum of American History." *Technology and Culture* 31 (2): 271–277.

Suttles, G. 1972. *The Social Construction of Communities.* Chicago: University of Chicago Press.

Taylor, J. C. 1976. *America as Art.* Washington, D.C.: Smithsonian Institution Press.

Thernstrom, S. 1965. "Yankee City Revisited: The Perils of Historical Naïveté." *American Sociological Review* 30 (1965): 234–242.

Thompson, P. 1967. *The Work of William Morris.* London: Heinemann.

Tuchman, G., A. K. Daniels, and J. Benet, eds. 1978. *Hearth and Home: Images of Women in the Mass Media.* New York: Oxford University Press.

Tuttle, C. 1992. "Buddhist Priests 2: Developers 1." *Places* 8 (1): 82–83.

Tweedale, G. 1992. "Steel Metropolis: A View of Sheffield Industry at Kelham Island Industrial Museum." *Technology and Culture* 33 (2): 328–335.

Urry, J. 1990. *The Tourist Gaze: Leisure and Travel in Contemporary Societies.* Newbury Park, Calif.: Sage Publications.

Vanderburgh, D. 1992. "Planning, Preservation and Polyculture." *Places* 8 (1): 32–41.

Varenne, H. 1977. *Americans Together: Structured Diversity in a Midwestern Town.* New York: Teachers' College Press.

Veblen, T. 1919. *The Theory of the Leisure Class: An Economic Study of Institutions.* New York: B. W. Huebsch.

West, B. 1988. "The Making of the English Working Past: A Critical View of the Ironbridge Gorge Museum." In *The Museum Time-Machine: Putting Culture on Display,* edited by R. Lumley. London: Routledge.

Widell, C. 1992. "Cultural Hurdles for Adaptive Re-Use of Historic Buildings in Japan." *Places* 8 (1): 80–82.

Williams, R. 1973. *The Country and the City.* New York: Oxford University Press.

———. 1983. *Culture and Society, 1780–1950.* New York: Columbia University Press.

———. 1989. *Resources of Hope: Culture, Democracy, Socialism.* Edited by R. Gable. London: Verso.

Wilson, R. 1992. "The Purpose of the Past." *Places* 8 (1): 46–57.

Wright, P. 1985. *On Living in an Old Country: The National Past in Contemporary Britain.* London: Verso.

Wuthnow, R. 1987. *Meaning and Moral Order: Explorations in Cultural Analysis.* Berkeley: University of California Press.

Yoshitomi, G. D. 1991. *Cultural Democracy. In Public Money & the Muse: Essays on Government Funding for the Arts.* Edited by S. Benedict. New York: W. W. Norton.

Zolberg, V. L. 1990. *Constructing a Sociology of the Arts.* Cambridge: Cambridge University Press.

Zukin, S. 1991. *Landscapes of Power: From Detroit to Disney World.* Berkeley: University of California Press.

INDEX

ABOUT THE AUTHOR

Diane Barthel is Professor of Sociology at the State University of New York, Stony Brook, New York. She received her doctorate from Harvard University, and, besides her affiliation with SUNY–Stony Brook, has also taught at Boston College and the University of Essex, as well as being Visiting Research Fellow at the Martin Centre for Architecture and Urban Studies, Cambridge. Her first book, *Amana: From Pietist Sect to American Community* was published in 1984 (University of Nebraska Press), and *Putting on Appearances: Gender and Advertising,* published by Temple University Press, appeared in 1988. Her research interests focus on the sociology of culture and the sociology of community.